HIDDEN HISTORY

PHILANTHROPY AT THE UNIVERSITY OF KENT

2015. 6.29

TRIONA FITTON
EDITED BY CATHY ROSS

Dear Mengwei,

Thank you so much for all your help!
You are truly a deserving Scholar.
Warm wishes,
Triona.

First Published 2015 by the University of Kent
Canterbury, Kent CT2 7NZ
United Kingdom

ISBN 978–1–902671–92–5

Copyright © Triona Fitton, 2015

Designed by Roland Codd – www.rols76.com
Illustrated map by Peter Gander – www.haveagander.biz
Printed by Pureprint Group Limited – www.pureprint.com
Principal photography by Matt Wilson for the University of Kent

Additional picture credits:
Ranald Mackechnie; Jim Higham; Simon Jarratt; Tim Stubbings; Discovery Park;
Triona Fitton; *inCant*; University of Kent Archives; British Cartoon Archive;
British Stand-Up Comedy Archive; Will Foster, Luke Lavan and Ellen Swift;
Kent Messenger; *Kentish Gazette*; Steve Double; EDA/Jason Dodd; Christian Richters

CONTENTS

Acknowledgements 4

Foreword 5

1 INTRODUCTION 6
The changing context since 1965 9
50 years of philanthropy 13

2 SETTING THE SCENE: A PHILANTHROPIC CAMPUS TOUR 14
Darwin College 15
The Colyer-Fergusson Building 16
The Gulbenkian Theatre 19
The Gulbenkian Cartouche 21
The Footsteps Project 23
Commemorative Benches 23
Cameron Court and Peter Stone 25
Rutherford College 25
Eliot College 29
The Jarman Building 32
Hymn 32
Huella Humana 34
Kent Sport 35
Synapse-Soleil 36

3 INCEPTION: THE BIRTH OF A UNIVERSITY 38
Location of the university 39
First fundraising efforts: courting industrial support 41
Second stage of fundraising efforts: the public appeal 45

4 EXCELLENCE: BUILDING A DISTINCTIVE UNIVERSITY 48
Supporting student excellence 49
Generation to generation scholarships 49
Memorial Scholarships 50
Music Scholarships 51
Sports Scholarships 52
The Medway Student Support Fund 53
International excellence 53
The University Library 56

5 INNOVATION: FORGING A PATHWAY FOR RESEARCH AND TEACHING 62
Original and unique collections 63
Innovative lectures 66
Establishing innovative areas of study 66
Innovation: A Chancellor's Role 68
Innovation: A Business Role 70

6 ENGAGEMENT: PHILANTHROPY ON AND OFF CAMPUS 72
Connection 1: Student journalism and the *Kent Messenger* 73
Connection 2: Women's Studies Students and the Canterbury Women's Refuge 75
Connection 3: Kent Union and local/distant communities 78
Connection 4: The University of Kent at Medway, local heritage and widening access 81
Connection 5: The Kent Law Campaign, the legal profession, serving the community 84

7 ENDOWMENT: LOOKING TO THE FUTURE 88
More philanthropy 89
More engaged philanthropy 90
More international philanthropy 92
Philanthropy: a never-ending history 93

Endnotes 94
Further reading 96

ACKNOWLEDGEMENTS

The Author would like to thank the following people for their help and advice in the production of *Hidden History*:

Dr Cathy Ross; Dr Beth Breeze; Michael Breeze; Geraldine Allinson; Stephen Burke; Dr Kate Bradley; James Bird; Professor Stephen Bann; Alison Coles; Sue Casement; Sonia Copeland-Bloom; Norma Clarke; Roland Codd; the staff of the Drill Hall Library; Paul Dyer; Hilary Edridge; Dr Jonathan Friday; Mary Fox; The Former Staff Association; Peter Gander; Steph Hughes; Mona Hodgetts; Graham Holmes; Cynthia Hawes; Fiona Jones; Professor Richard Jones; Sir Charles Jessel; Dr Peter Klappa; Anne Lyttle and Gillian Orman from Rising Sun; Dr Luke Lavan; Professor Keith Mander; Ann MacDonald and the Special Collections team; Michael Mills; Louise Naylor; Billy Ng; Anna Pollard; Robin Pitman; Professor Jan Pahl; Jenny Richardson; Alison Rees at the Nuffield Foundation; The Rochester Bridge Trust; Professor Colin Seymour-Ure; Sophie Scott; Dr Ben Thomas; Mengwei Tu; Susan Wanless.

FOREWORD

2015 is a special year for the University of Kent. We are celebrating 50 years since our Royal Charter in 1965, and that offers an opportunity for reflection on what those 50 years have brought to the university, its staff, students, and the surrounding county.

The university has grown considerably since 1965, and the important role that philanthropy has played in this has never been truly celebrated. This book endeavours to correct this by revealing the hidden history of gifts to the University of Kent. It will demonstrate the ways in which philanthropy aided the initial formation of a university in Kent, and how it has contributed to the development of the campus, continued excellence and innovation in teaching and research, and a bright future for all those involved with the work of the university, including those in the local community within which we are now embedded.

This book recounts some of the most interesting and evocative tales of philanthropic gifts to our university which, over 50 years, may have otherwise been lost to the sands of time. We hope that it will also act as a beacon for future fundraising: illustrating the importance of philanthropic funding for higher education as we head towards our 100th anniversary.

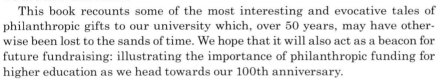

Professor Dame Julia Goodfellow, Vice-Chancellor

INTRODUCTION

Spring 2015. A student emerges from a lecture. She finds a bench with a beautiful view over the cathedral city of Canterbury, and sits to eat a sandwich before heading to the Templeman Library. Though she doesn't notice it, the bench has a shiny plaque naming a colleague in whose honour the seat was installed many years ago, paid for by admiring colleagues and friends. There are many such benches on the campus, all of them small examples of the 'hidden history' of philanthropy.

The student is also a music scholar. Without her scholarship, paid for by donations from alumni and friends of the University of Kent, she might have had to abandon her studies. Her lecture was held in a building funded by a major donor. The academic who gave the lecture is working on research funded by a charitable trust. The library she will soon be working in has been stocked with many volumes donated by supporters of the university.

These are examples of the 'everyday philanthropy' that goes largely uncelebrated, but has been an important part of daily life at campus for the past 50 years – and will be for the foreseeable future. This book shines a spotlight on the hidden history of philanthropy at the University of Kent, revealing how the voluntary contributions of private donors have played an essential part in our establishment. These have enhanced our environment, enabled excellence and innovation in research and teaching, and are manifested in ongoing engagement with the community beyond campus.

The idea of universities receiving funding from philanthropic sources is often attributed to the United States, where private financing of higher education is more widely understood and accepted as a 'good thing'. Many US universities are named after the original donor: famous examples include John Harvard, Jane Stanford and Ezra Cornell. Yet on both sides of the Atlantic, and indeed in other countries around the world, gifts from private donors have always played a role in funding academic excellence, building extra-curricular facilities and widening access to higher education.

Below The view from the university down towards Canterbury

> **"**
> Philanthropy
> has helped shape
> the institution's
> character and
> achievements
> every step of
> the way.

British universities are popularly understood to be institutions whose financial support comes primarily from the state, with the role of philanthropy being restricted to paying for 'nice-to-have' extras, rather than helping deliver core parts of the educational programme. Such an impression is misleading. A closer look at the University of Kent reveals that philanthropy has helped shape the institution's character and achievements every step of the way. Private donations have played a role from the very earliest efforts to build a university in the county, to today's mission to be 'the UK's European University'. Philanthropy is central to the Kent story, and this book charts its hidden history.

The history of philanthropy at the University of Kent includes small and big gifts, and help that has been given and received. The university has received support from many different sources, ranging from gifts of tree saplings to multimillion-pound donations, from books provided by local residents to stock the newly-built library to the time spent by students volunteering to help local abused women. The story is about much more than cash, and involves a reciprocal relationship with the world beyond our campuses. Philanthropy at Kent is about engagement and inspiration; about working with individuals and communities on common endeavours; and about demonstrating our values and building enduring relationships. The countless benefits derived from these gifts have come to define our university; beginning back in the 1950s, when the University of Kent existed as an idea and a dream.

Before World War II, Britain's higher education provision largely consisted of two earlier generations of universities: the medieval foundations at Oxford and Cambridge, and the 19th-century 'red brick' civic universities located in urban centres. Both types of university had traditions of philanthropic endowments, with income streams of various sizes flowing from individuals, alumni, affluent manufacturers, local businesses and civic groups. Local pride and local benefit played a strong role in generating the philanthropy on which these earlier universities depended. Before the war, British universities only received half their income from public sources.[1]

Types of university in the United Kingdom		
Type	**Description**	**Examples**
Ancient Universities	Medieval or Renaissance institutions.	**University of Oxford** – founded in 1096 **University of Cambridge** – founded 1209 **University of St Andrews** – founded 1413
Civic universities (also known as 'red brick' universities)	Institutions founded in major UK cities to support industrial and economic growth	**University of Birmingham** – founded 1875 **University of Bristol** – founded 1876 **University of Leeds** – founded 1906
Plate-glass universities (also known as 'campus' universities)	Campus-based universities intended to provide more student places and boost economic growth	**University of Sussex** – founded 1961 **University of York** – founded 1963 **University of Kent** – founded 1965
Post-1992 universities (also known as 'new universities')	Former polytechnics or further education colleges granted university status in the early 1990s	**University of the West of England** – founded in 1595 as the Bristol Society of Merchant Venturers' Navigation School **University of Huddersfield** – founded as a science and technical college in 1825 **University of Westminster** – founded in 1838 as the Royal Polytechnic Institution

Left Students arriving to study at the University of Kent, 1965

The University of Kent is one of the new, or 'plate-glass', universities built in the 1960s as a result of the post-war vision of greatly expanded higher education in Britain. This vision predicted a 21st-century Britain with more students, a wider geographical spread of universities across the country, and higher levels of academic achievement in the population as a whole.

The 1944 Education Act led to a threefold expansion of student numbers, from 69,000 students in 1938–9, to 216,000 in 1962–3.[2] The Robbins Report of 1963 highlighted the substantial shortfall of places for qualified school-leavers.[3] This prediction was already common knowledge by the late 1950s, when efforts to identify sites for new higher education institutions began in earnest, and when dreamers in Kent began to share their ambitions for the county to host a new university.

A crucial criterion for deciding the location of the plate-glass universities was 'ample evidence of strong local support' and 'an assurance of substantial financial support'.[4] The extent and nature of local support in Kent underlines the fact that, despite the role of government in planning the new universities as a national programme, local philanthropic support was essential to the plan's delivery. Whilst the amounts of philanthropic support for universities has ebbed and flowed over time, the significance of philanthropy has persisted and private donations have continued to play a key – if largely unsung – role in university finances and campus life.

THE CHANGING CONTEXT SINCE 1965

The new universities of the 1960s succeeded in accommodating rising student numbers, which more than doubled to 463,000 in 1971, and reached 526,000 by 1981.[5] Since the 1980s a new policy climate has brought new questions about what levels of funding higher education might expect from the state, and many British universities began to look to sources other than government for their funding needs. Philanthropy was once more back on the agenda, and Kent was not alone in trying to build a more proactive fundraising culture among staff and students.

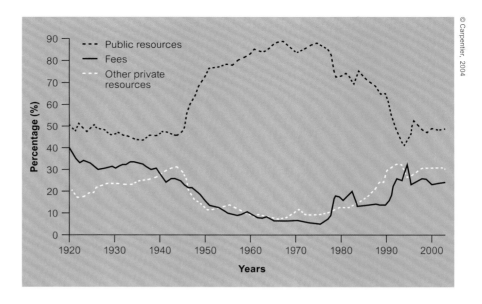

Right Figure 1. Income Structure of Universities in the United Kingdom,[6] 1921–2003

University of Kent
£1 million+ donors

Historic donations adjusted to take account of inflation:
- Princess Marina, Duchess of Kent, and the Royal Family
- Pfizer Ltd
- Professor Ibnu Sutowo
- Sir James Colyer-Fergusson
- Rochester Bridge Trust
- The Football Foundation
- The Colyer-Fergusson Charitable Trust
- The Honourable Charles Wigoder

Kent's first alumni relations programme, *Kent Society*, was established in 1983. This was a membership organisation offering events and publications in return for an annual subscription. The university appointed a development officer and research assistant in 1989 – the Development Department grew out of this, and continues to fundraise for Kent to this day. *Kent Society* was dissolved in 1994, and replaced with an alumni programme that did not require paid membership, thus widening the pool of potential alumni donors.

Alumni engagement programmes are a mainstay of successful university fundraising in the UK. As Figure 1 shows, it has become increasingly necessary for universities to find new funding sources since the early 1990s. In 1998, the introduction of tuition fees buoyed university income a little, with students being required to pay £1,000 per year for their higher education, dependent upon their family income. Despite a significant rise in tuition fees in 2004, and again in 2012 up to a maximum of £9,000 per year, university income still depends essentially on government grants; however, the proportion from private donations is growing, due in part to active encouragement from government in the form of tax relief for donations and match-funding schemes. The Thomas Report on higher education (2004) further encouraged universities to become 'asking institutions', recommending that they develop fundraising strategies and make best use of the giving incentives on offer. By 2012, philanthropic income at 152 UK universities totalled £693 million, a rise of 35% since 2006–7.[7]

The decision to diversify university income further has introduced new debates into academic life: about whether, for example, dependence on external benefactors might jeopardise academic freedom or damage institutional reputations.[8] However, the drive to build relationships with local businesses, friends, and alumni has also brought benefits. For the University of Kent, philanthropic activity over the past 50 years has been crucial in building relationships with external supporters, both individual and corporate. As explored in more detail later, many of these relationships proved to be long-term, and some of the university's founding benefactors remain deeply involved in the institution's development to this day.

This chapter gives an overview of the financial context experienced by universities over the past half century, and outlines of how Kent has responded. Chapter 2 sets off on a tour of the university's original, and largest, campus in Canterbury, noting some of the biggest and most interesting philanthropic sites to be found on every corner. Chapter 3 describes the role that philanthropy played in the establishment of the university, highlighting some of the key people and milestones of the fundraising appeal needed to turn the vision into reality. Chapter 4 explains how philanthropic funding has helped ensure the university achieves excellence in research and teaching, and Chapter 5 shows the role that private funding has played in ensuring ongoing innovation at the university. Chapter 6 looks at how the University of Kent has engaged with local community and business over time. The final chapter looks to the future and suggests how philanthropy could play a role in the next 50 years at Kent.

This book is a celebration of the many facets of 50 years of philanthropy at the University of Kent. Revealing the 'hidden history' of philanthropy is an unending task, as gifts are given to the university almost daily. In this short study it is impossible to mention every donation by name: however, the selection included here illustrates just how fundamental philanthropy has been in shaping the university's life and values. The story of philanthropy at the University of Kent is not just an account of the past but a celebration of the generosity of spirit generated by the university, now and for the future.

Below Aerial view of the University of Kent Canterbury campus, 2013

50 YEARS OF PHILANTHROPY

1959
May: Kent Education Committee begin plans for a University in Kent

1960
May: Donation of £50,000 from Pfizer Ltd

June: Lord Bossom holds the first fundraising luncheon

November: Canterbury site chosen

1962
August: Geoffrey Templeman appointed as Vice-Chancellor

October: Donations total £375,000

1963
January: Princess Marina becomes the first Chancellor of the University of Kent

October: Robbins Report on Higher Education released

1965
January: The University of Kent at Canterbury officially established by Royal Charter

May: Donations total £450,000

June: Public foundation fund appeal launches

October: The 'First 500' students arrive

Eliot College opens

December: *inCant* launches

1966
June: Donations total £563,000

October: Rutherford College opens

1967
October: W. H. Auden gives the first Eliot Lecture

1968
Templeman Library opens

October: Keynes College opens

1969
June: The Gulbenkian Theatre opens

1970
October: Darwin College opens

1972
November: First Keynes Lecture

1973
November: Centre for the Study of Cartoons and Caricature opens

1974
July: Collapse of south-west corner of Cornwallis building

1975
October: Students and staff set up the Women's Refuge in Canterbury

1983
Kent Society (the first alumni group) launches

1984
September: Peter Stone Heather Garden created

1988
Development Department opens

1997
October: Bridge Warden's College opens

2003
University of Kent at Canterbury is renamed 'The University of Kent'

2004
May: Thomas Report on Increasing Voluntary Giving to Higher Education released

2005
October: Medway Campus opens

2008
November: Centre for Philanthropy launches

2009
October: Sports Pavilion opens

2012
November: Eliot College receives bust of T. S. Eliot

December: Colyer-Fergusson Building opens

2013
June: British Stand-Up Comedy Archive launches

November: Kent Law Campaign launches

2014
June: Footsteps Project launches

2015
University of Kent's 50th Anniversary

2
SETTING THE SCENE
A PHILANTHROPIC CAMPUS TOUR

The physical environment of the University of Kent has changed significantly over time, and the presence of philanthropy is visible in the buildings and general surroundings that staff and students encounter every day on campus. For example, the Gulbenkian Theatre would not exist without funding received from the Calouste Gulbenkian Foundation in 1969. The theatre is a good example of the richness that philanthropy has brought to Kent – not only in furthering the university's aspirations to encourage innovation in the arts, but also contributing to community engagement. The theatre's original slogan was 'On campus, but not off limits!'

From the first donations of books to the university library, when it was housed above a shop in Canterbury city centre, to the saplings planted by the Kent Men of the Trees, philanthropy across campus is ubiquitous. This chapter takes a leisurely stroll around some of the most striking sights, and highlights a few 'everyday' examples of philanthropy. These include things that people might pass by without appreciating what they embody: trees or benches commemorating loved ones; buildings; and works of art that brighten the campus walkways.

FIRST STOP: DARWIN COLLEGE

We begin our tour in Darwin College, where many philanthropic gifts are safely kept within the Master's office on the first floor. Numerous paintings were received by donation, including one by John Collier of Charles Darwin himself. This was given by Maidstone donor Jack Johns, who also gave a prestigious collection of books by and about Charles Darwin to the college library.

Eventually the college library was subsumed into the main Templeman Library, but Darwin College retained the portrait of its namesake. It is a copy of a portrait completed in 1881 for the Linnean Society, to mark the reading of the Darwin-Wallace papers on the theory of evolution by natural selection in the Society's rooms in 1858.[9]

Adjacent to the Collier portrait is another donation: a painting that resembles Darwin College (although 'not an exact likeness', according to Darwin College Master Jonathan Friday). It was painted by Michael Hunt and given in 1971 by the college architect, H. Faulkner Brown.

Above Portrait of Charles Darwin by John Collier (1883)

Left Painting of Darwin College by Michael Hunt

Above Bust of Erasmus Darwin

Another early gift housed in the Master's office is a photographic portrait of Darwin given to the college by George Darwin, great-grandson of Charles Darwin. The photograph was taken by Julia Margaret Cameron, a prestigious Victorian photographer. The Darwin family has close associations with the college, and in the early 1970s permitted the college to use the family coat of arms. They also donated a bust of Erasmus Darwin, Charles Darwin's grandfather and a notable physician in his own right; the bust now presides over the bar in Origins, the college restaurant.

Beside the Cameron portrait of Darwin lies a first edition of Darwin's *Expression of the Emotions in Man and Animals*, donated by two of the college's senior members in May 1973. Also in the office is a print by Polly Keith-Lucas, the daughter of the first Master of Darwin College, Professor Bryan Keith-Lucas.

As you step outside, note the now fully-grown tree, given to the College by the Kent Association of Parish Councils in honour of the 1973 United Nations Tree Year. Now, head toward greener philanthropic pastures…

NEXT STOP: THE COLYER-FERGUSSON BUILDING

In 2012, the University of Kent opened a magnificent new music building and concert hall. The £8 million complex was named after the benefactor Sir James Colyer-Fergusson and the Colyer-Fergusson Charitable Trust. The initial vision of a state-of-the-art music building came from the Director of Music, Susan Wanless, who together with Deputy Vice-Chancellor, Professor Keith Mander and then Director of Development Joanna Motion, believed that provision for music practice and performance on campus was sorely lacking.

Following Sir James's death in 2004, Susan learned that he had bequeathed one-sixth of his estate to the university, representing a further donation of £1 million, to support music on campus. The relationship with Colyer-Fergusson did not end there. A relationship developed with Sir James's cousin, Jonathan Monckton, the chair of the Colyer-Fergusson Charitable Trust. Jonathan 'appreciated the university's immense pride in being associated with Sir James,' says Susan, 'and our genuine desire to keep his name alive'. Jonathan Monckton was a regular attendee of the Cathedral concerts bearing his cousin's name, and presented the Colyer-Fergusson Music Prize every year.

Below The Colyer-Fergusson Building

© Christian Richters

In November 2008, Susan Wanless and Professor Mander launched an appeal to raise funds for a new music building on the Canterbury campus. Jonathan Monckton was invited to a lecture and dinner when the appeal launch was announced. 'As we walked across campus to the dinner,' Susan recalls, 'he said to me "How much do you need?" When I bravely suggested seven million pounds, he simply said "OK, send me a note".'

With this encouraging response, the university made a formal funding request to the trustees of the Colyer-Fergusson Charitable Trust. In February 2009, only 12 weeks after the appeal was launched, the Trust offered £4.5 million, followed by a further £700,000 at a later date. Together with Sir James's original £1 million legacy, match-funding from the Higher Education Funding Council, and more than 200 donations from other benefactors, the construction of a dedicated concert hall and suite of practice rooms was made possible.

SIR JAMES COLYER-FERGUSSON

During his lifetime, Sir James Colyer-Fergusson had been an accomplished pianist, a theatre and concert enthusiast, and a generous philanthropist to the arts. He supported the musical life of the university in many ways, including giving a £110,000 endowment in 1996, when he also gave £52,000 towards the refurbishment of the Gulbenkian Theatre. The university honoured his gifts by holding annual classical music concerts bearing his name. The Colyer-Fergusson Music Prize for outstanding student contribution to the organisation of music on campus was established in acknowledgement of his generosity, following his death in 2004.

'Sir James's generosity had an immediate impact on the cultural life of the university,' Susan Wanless explains. 'It has enabled the development of student music-making, and allowed me to be far more adventurous in my programming, removing the element of financial insecurity which invariably accompanies creative projects.'

> " Sir James was a wonderfully kind and gentle man who took a great personal interest in our music-making, attending concerts whenever he could.
> Susan Wanless,
> Director of Music

Above Sir James Colyer-Fergusson

Susan Wanless says, 'My relationships with Sir James, Jonathan Monckton and the Colyer-Fergusson Charitable Trust have evolved over the past two decades. I have been so lucky to have such enthusiastic and committed benefactors, and it has always been a delight to involve them in all our musical project and events.'

Along with Sir James and the charitable trust that continues his philanthropic work, the many generous benefactors of the Colyer-Fergusson building are named, in gilt lettering, in the music building's foyer. These benefactors include: the Sir Charles Jessel Charitable Trust; James Bird, a Deputy Lieutenant of Kent and former University Treasurer; the actor Orlando Bloom; and Bloom's mother and sister, the author Sonia Copeland-Bloom and actress Samantha Bloom.

The Colyer-Fergusson Building opened with a gala celebration on 8 December 2012. 'It has transformed the musical life of our students, staff, and local community,' says Susan, 'It's an extraordinary facility; a sought after venue with wonderful acoustics.' Many local choirs, orchestras and schools now perform regularly in the hall and it is also the venue for concerts by internationally-acclaimed musicians. The practice rooms are also in great demand with around 200 students using them each year.

'It's all to do with enhancing student experience,' says Susan. The foyer, which contains a smaller stage for informal performances, connects to the Gulbenkian Theatre, next stop on this philanthropic tour.

> Music is very close to my heart, and the university has been good to me over the years. I gave because I wanted to thank the university, and because I want the people of East Kent to enjoy the Arts as much as possible.
>
> James Bird, donor to the new Colyer-Fergusson Music Building

Opposite page Practising in the Colyer-Fergusson Building

NEXT STOP: THE GULBENKIAN THEATRE

The Gulbenkian Theatre was opened in 1969 to much fanfare. From the beginning, the university saw the Gulbenkian's role as a community arts and theatre complex, complementing Canterbury's Marlowe Theatre. Its programming encompasses a variety of tastes and art forms – from hard rock music legends like AC/DC, kitchen-sink drama plays like 'A Taste of Honey' and classic musicals such as 'Grease', to local productions from amateur groups and the university's drama society; all have graced the stage at the Gulbenkian.

One of the founding professors of English at the University of Kent, Reg A. Foakes, played a crucial role in persuading the Gulbenkian Foundation to fund the theatre.[10] In 1966, the university was still very new, and keen to establish itself as a site of innovative arts and cultural activities. To do so, it would need a building that could serve a variety of purposes. Besides playing a role in literary studies on campus, through providing facilities for plays, rehearsing and teaching, the aspiration for the theatre was also to enrich cultural life in Canterbury more generally, bringing together the university and the local community. The Gulbenkian Foundation agreed to fund a third of the cost of the theatre, giving the university £35,000 (the equivalent of over £600,000 in 2015), and the building its unusual name.

The rest of the money was secured by the first Registrar of the university, Eric Fox, in an appeal to the University Grants Committee (UGC). A change was made to the original architectural design, which incorporated a cluster of hexagonal buildings detached from other buildings. This was found to be too expensive, so the Gulbenkian was attached to the adjacent Cornwallis

THE CALOUSTE GULBENKIAN FOUNDATION

Calouste Gulbenkian was born in 1869, the son of a rich Armenian oil baron. Known for funding many Armenian churches and schools, he became a British citizen in 1902 and began to distribute his wealth in Britain as well as in the Ottoman Kingdom. Gulbenkian was a self-styled 'business architect'[11] – he wasn't interested in solely buying and selling, but in furthering the potential of business through investment in scholarships, hospitals, libraries and culture. By the time of his death in 1955, he had established one of the largest foundations in the world. It continues to fund cultural projects across Europe to this day.

Below The Gulbenkian Theatre

building with the intention of saving the cost for one wall, and sharing toilet facilities and a café with the existing lecture theatre.

The Gulbenkian Theatre, with its eye-catching octagonal architecture, 342-person capacity and lively programme of events, remains an important hub for the arts on campus and for the local community. Visitor numbers regularly exceed 30,000 per year.

NEXT STOP: THE GULBENKIAN CARTOUCHE

On the back of the Gulbenkian Theatre is an imposing vision – a coat of arms flanked by a lion and a unicorn. Due to its location, it is often overlooked by busy theatre-goers hunting for a parking space. Yet the Gulbenkian cartouche has a wonderful, hidden history.

The cartouche contains George III's Royal Coat of Arms. Prior to 1800, the Royal Arms featured three French fleur-de-lys in the top right-hand quarter, alongside the three lions for England, a white horse for Scotland, the stringed harp of Ireland, and a final quartile representing George I's ancestral history in Hanover, Germany, and the Imperial Crown of the Holy Roman Empire. The imagery of the fleur-de-lys was removed from the Royal Arms after 1800, when France became a republic. This makes the Gulbenkian cartouche over 200 years old.

The cartouche was originally on the wall of the Ipswich barracks, built in 1793 at a time when William Pitt's government were preparing to meet the French invasion. Later, it was moved to the old Infantry Barracks at Canterbury. When the demolition of the Canterbury Barracks was scheduled in 1967, the cartouche was due to be thrown away.

Professor Bryan Keith-Lucas, the first Master of Darwin College (and later President of *Kent Society*, the original university alumni group), was formerly a member of the Queen's Own Buffs, Royal East Kent Regiment, and was still in close contact with members of the regiment when it merged with three others to form the Queen's Regiment in 1966. When Professor Keith-Lucas discovered that the cartouche was going to be put in a skip, 'He said in a trice, "well, the university will have it!"' recalls Colin Seymour-Ure, Emeritus Professor of Politics. 'And there it has been since.'

Left The cartouche on the back of the Gulbenkian Theatre, containing the Royal Arms of George III

Professor Keith-Lucas's rescue of this 18th-century relic underlines the enterprising spirit of many of the early staff and students at the university. It also illustrates a form of philanthropy that bypasses the giving of money, yet is equally valuable – the giving of time and effort. Maintenance of the cartouche has also generated further philanthropy. In the 1980s, the unicorn's nose had become dislodged due to bad weather; *Kent Society* sponsored the restoration, using funds raised by alumni.

Adjacent to the Gulbenkian Theatre stands *Father Courage*, a sculpture by Frederick Edward McWilliam (1960). Paid for by funds from the Gulbenkian Foundation, the title refers to Bertold Brecht's play *Mother Courage*.[12] The piece echoes Brecht's concerns with human struggle and war: themes that are found in other works by McWilliam, an Irish sculptor from County Down, whose work is held by many major art galleries around the world.

Below F. E. McWilliam's *Father Courage* sculpture (1960)

NEXT STOP: THE FOOTSTEPS PROJECT

In front of *Father Courage* is Kent's newest philanthropic landmark: The
Footsteps Project. This celebration of the university's 50th anniversary is a
work in progress. It takes the form of a path made up of bricks engraved
with messages from students and staff, past and present, together with other
people associated with the university over the past 50 years. The path is
designed to look like a railway line, and thus commemorates the Canterbury
and Whitstable 'Crab and Winkle Line', which ran beneath this part of the
university grounds. The location of the former railway tunnel underneath
the campus caused an infamous collapse of the south-west corner of the
Cornwallis building in July 1974.[13]

Each 'footstep' brick marks at least a £50 donation to the Kent Opportunity
Fund – a university initiative which funds many student scholarships, bursaries and research. The enduring legacy of the fond memories displayed
amongst the bricks will also act as a contribution to future opportunities and
progress, allowing future students to walk in the footsteps of those who were
here before.

NEXT STOP: COMMEMORATIVE BENCHES

Just to the right of the Rutherford causeway, outside the student rooms and
facing the Senate and the University Library, is a bench with an inscription.
A large number of commemorative benches and trees dot the campus at
Canterbury. Many are placed on the crest of the hillside behind Eliot College,
taking advantage of the beautiful view over Canterbury and the Cathedral.

Each bench and tree has a unique story behind it: some commemorate loved
ones, others honour academic contributions. This particular bench represents
both categories. It is visited and maintained every year by the sister and
friends of Graham Clarke, in whose honour the bench was installed.

Above A selection of commemorative plaques from across campus

Right Norma Clarke on the bench dedicated to the memory of her brother, Professor Graham Clarke

Graham was Emeritus Professor of Photography and Visual Arts at the University of Kent, where he had worked from 1974 until 2007. His academic interest originally lay in North American art and literature. He fostered many of Kent's transatlantic links, teaching and researching at the Universities of Colorado, Brown, Yale and Connecticut.

When Professor Clarke died aged only 58, his sister Norma and brother Roy wanted to mark his life and work at the university in a physical way. Norma explains:

> 'We were so proud of Graham. His achievements in his academic career were exemplary. It was important to the family to have a special memorial for Graham, so we decided to place a bench in the grounds of the university, which seemed fitting to commemorate his many years of dedication, commitment and success at the university.
>
> 'Roy and I organised and funded the bench, which I visit every year on Graham's birthday and on the anniversary of his death. It gives me great comfort, as I feel close both to him and my brother Roy, who played such a huge part in Graham's life and sadly passed away only two years after Graham died. I leave flowers as a mark of remembrance, love and respect.
>
> 'Both Graham and Roy are very much missed. The world is a lesser place without them.'

The significance of these benches, and the trees that are planted in honour or memory of an individual, is often overlooked, despite being an integral part of the university's landscape. They speak of the university as a collective undertaking, enriched over time by the contributions of hundreds of individuals – former staff, students and friends.

NEXT STOP: CAMERON COURT AND PETER STONE

As students rush past on their way from their rooms to the library, it is easy to overlook the small plaques and nameplates that sit beside the pathways. One such plaque lies just outside Rutherford, not far from Professor Clarke's bench. This commemorates Dr Peter Stone, Senior Lecturer in English, who died in 1984.

Above The plaque commemorating the Dr Peter Stone Heather Garden

The Peter Stone Heather Garden was a small collection of ornamental heather plants, which Dr Stone's colleagues, students, friends and family clubbed together to fund as a tribute to the influential Shakespearean scholar. The BBC radio presenter Charlotte Green, a former student, remembers Dr Stone as 'unceasingly courteous, chivalrous and compassionate': 'Whenever I see [Shakespeare] plays performed or read them at home, I think of Dr Stone and how good he was at conveying his own love of Shakespeare to his students.'[14]

The Peter Stone memorial was recently relocated to beside the English Department, in a garden known as 'Cameron Court'. The space was named after the first Master of Rutherford College, Professor James Cameron, who presided over the college from 1967 until 1971.

NEXT STOP: RUTHERFORD COLLEGE

The next stop on the philanthropic tour is Rutherford College, named after Ernest Rutherford, the prominent nuclear physicist and Nobel Prize-winner who established the nuclear structure of the atom. Entering the courtyard, visitors see a seating area with a bronze bust of Lord Rutherford. The bust was commissioned from the artist Frederic Deane, and paid for by the college's senior members.[15] Another cast of the piece stands in the Rutherford Library at the University of Manchester. The bust was valued in 2010 at roughly £2,000.

Lean and loafe at your ease...

An interpretation of Walt Whitman's *Song of Myself* (1892), used to publicise the new Rutherford seating area in October 1997

The seating in Rutherford's central courtyard also speaks to the impact of philanthropy. Designed and built to honour the college's 30th year, it was paid for in part by the Development Fund, which raises money from alumni, and in part by donations from senior and honorary college members, responding to a direct appeal from the Master. The renovated seating area cost over £1,600, and was installed in an inaugural ceremony in October 1997. Every day students and staff relax in the Rutherford courtyard, unaware of the philanthropy that surrounds them.

Left Rutherford seating plaque

RUTHERFORD COLLEGE

This seating was erected in celebration of the College's 30th Anniversary and paid for with generous donations from staff, honorary members, friends and the Development Fund.

Summer 1997

Above left Chinese Tapestries

Above right Keith Vaughan gouache

Below Archibald Ziegler painting

Inside Rutherford, further examples of philanthropy can be found. Adorning the walls of the Stanley Rogers Room – named after the college's first Bursar, who was appointed in 1966 – are a pair of beautiful Chinese tapestries, gifts from Professor Vivienne Mylne, a senior college member and Professor of French. The fund for framing these was a philanthropic gift from another senior member of the college, Professor George Curry.

Below in the Rutherford Senior Common Room, a gouache by Sussex-born neo-romantic artist Keith Vaughan hangs on the wall. This work was paid for by the Gulbenkian Foundation.

On the other side of the Senior Common Room is a painting by London-based artist Archibald Ziegler. An unidentified family member had previously attended the University of Kent, and gave the painting after his death in 1971. The university received six Zieglers in total: two of these, a nude and a landscape, sit either side of the windows in Rutherford dining hall.

The dining hall is a cavernous room which contains a striking portrait of Nelson Mandela by South African artist Janet Wilson. The college's senior members raised £1,050 to pay for the portrait, which is a huge, silkscreen collage created from A4-sized prints placed in a grid. Janet Wilson is also a top-ranking sportswoman in her home country, having competed and come first in the World Rowing Championships in 1996. She was visiting the UK from Johannesburg with her husband Dr Gregory Mills, Director of the South African Institute of International Affairs, who was a visiting fellow in the Politics and International Relations department at the University of Kent at the time.

The portrait continues to provide inspiration to students in the Politics and International Relations department, which is housed within Rutherford College.

Philanthropy also comes from students who want to leave their mark on the university when they graduate. Facing the window of Rutherford's dining hall are four large neo-expressionist paintings and a diptych by Kent Fine Art graduate Stephen Dorsett. They are on permanent loan from the artist following an exhibition of the works when he graduated in 2005. These

'abstract form' works, along with the other art displayed here, are a bright contrast to Rutherford's dark 1960s décor. Dorsett comments, 'I am proud to have my paintings displayed in such an auspicious place.'

Rutherford College has a fine selection of silver items that were donated as gifts, although these are not on current display. The collection includes four silver gilt water jugs – a gift from the Company of Goldsmiths in 1971 – and a silver goblet given by the first Master, James Cameron.

From Rutherford, if we turn left and walk past a bench commemorating Kent's 40th Anniversary in 2005 (beneath which lies a time capsule which will be opened in 2045), we come to the Eliot Causeway.

Above left Janet Wilson's portrait of Nelson Mandela

Above right Three Stephen Dorsett paintings

Below Silver gilt Goldsmiths jug, belonging to Eliot College

THE GOLDSMITH'S COMPANY

In the 1960s and early 1970s, the Goldsmith's Company of London commissioned recent graduates to produce a set of silver gilt water jugs for each of the 'new universities'. Each of the early colleges was given four jugs for use during High Table dinners, engraved with 'The gift of the Worshipful Company of Goldsmiths'. Darwin College receiving the final set in March 1971.[16]

Each jug carries the university's early coat of arms, featuring three Kentish Choughs (from the coat of arms of St Thomas Becket, Archbishop of Canterbury, and also used on the Canterbury coat of arms) above the 'White Horse of Kent', an image that has represented the county for over 1,000 years.

ENDURING TIES: SIR GEORGE JESSEL, SIR CHARLES JESSEL AND THE JESSEL FAMILY TRUST

The relationship between the Jessel family and the University of Kent began with a £1,441 donation to the University Foundation Fund in 1965 by the late Sir George Jessel. His son, Sir Charles Jessel, also later donated £1,441 to the Foundation Fund.

The Jessel family's involvement was not only financial. In 1966, Sir Charles and two of his staff, who worked as tractor drivers, helped deliver manure and plant trees around the newly-built Eliot College. This *pro bono* gardening service prompted a dispute with the campus architect, who was determined that Eliot College would be surrounded by wych elm trees. Sir Charles advised against this, saying that trees with such large boughs were liable to fall in the event of a serious storm. In a freak storm of 1967, this is precisely what occurred, prompting Sir Charles to return a year later with the local conservation group Kent Men of the Trees, and plant more saplings for free on the university site.

In recent years, Sir Charles has also contributed to the university's Music Scholarships scheme through his family's charitable trust. 'I was so fortunate to go to university at a time when it didn't cost anything to go,' he explains. 'I went twice, in 1942 and 1946, to Oxford University, and I feel very privileged to have had that opportunity. I support music scholars through my charitable trust as I would like other people to have the same experience.'

Below Trees outside Eliot College, 2015

NEXT STOP: ELIOT COLLEGE

Much of the philanthropy present in Eliot College has a strong provenance due to ties to its namesake, the author T. S. Eliot. But some is as deeply embedded within the campus environment. The renovated seating area and lighting within the Eliot courtyard was installed in memory of Alex 'Sandy' Brown, a Physics alumnus who left a gift to his college when he passed away in 2007. A plaque above the exit to the Eliot causeway commemorates the opening of the refurbished courtyard. Dr Michael Hughes, Master of Eliot at that time, said:

Above Eliot courtyard plaque

> *'Sandy Brown was the first in his family to attend university and he gained a great deal from his experience at the University of Kent and from his time at Eliot College in particular. It is a moving tribute and an indication of his priorities and nature that at the end of his life he remembered the college and those who live and work here.'*

Further into the building is the Eliot dining hall – the vast space where the first degrees were conferred by Kent's earliest Chancellor, Princess Marina. On either side of the raised stage area at the back of the wall are two large, panelled works of art.

The mural on the left came from the NatWest bank in Canterbury, and was originally drawn by Canterbury College of Art in 1956. It charts the history of commerce from Roman times up until the 1950s. The imagery comes from a number of sources including the Eadwine Psalter, the Luttrell Psalter, and the Ellesmere Manuscript. A member of the Buffs East Kent Regiment

Below Natwest Mural

SILVERWARE

The college also has a significant collection of silverware that was donated. There are four silver armada dishes, given by the Queen's Own Buffs Royal Kent Regiment in 1966. A fine selection of silver cutlery and other tableware, made by Ramsden & Carr, were also donated by the regiment. A silver candelabra inscribed as being 'Presented by Kent County Council to the University of Kent, 1966' is also in the collection, along with a dish from G. S. Darlowe, the first librarian.

Above Bust of T. S. Eliot
by Jacob Epstein

Right A selection of first
edition T. S. Eliot books
given to the college

ENDURING TIES: VALERIE ELIOT

The relationship between Valerie Eliot, the widow of T. S. Eliot, and the university's first college was indeed special. It lasted from 1965 until her death in 2012, and is an eloquent example of philanthropy working on a long timescale. Valerie Eliot supported the university in many ways, including a generous gift in 1994 that enabled the creation of a dedicated poetry room in the library. But the object that most embodies the warmth of the relationship is the bust by Jacob Epstein that now stands in Eliot College.

The university had long wanted to mark the Eliot connection through an appropriate image of the poet. In 1965 Professor Alec Whitehouse, the first Master of Eliot College, wrote to Valerie Eliot, soon after her husband's death:

> 'We have been concerned right from the beginning, about the possibilities of having in the college a portrait, photograph or bust of Mr Eliot. We have proceeded slowly for various reasons: finance being one, and suitable locations being another.'

One of the suggestions for memorialising Eliot was to make a copy of Jacob Epstein's bust of the poet. Valerie Eliot replied that this was not possible, regretfully, as only nine casts were taken from the mould, and Epstein's estate would not allow further casts to be made. But on 4 July 1970, Valerie Eliot wrote to the Master of Eliot College that she was redrafting her will 'in which I shall leave the Epstein bust of my husband to the college, as I promised [Professor Alec] Whitehouse'.

The college kept in close touch with Valerie Eliot and the current Master of Eliot College, Stephen Burke, attended her funeral in 2012. There, Eliot's executors told him that Valerie had not changed her will and the bust was indeed to come to Eliot College. Thus, after almost 50 years of waiting, the University of Kent inherited this valuable and significant work of art. It was, as Stephen Burke stated, an 'amazing acquisition'.

Eliot College is in possession of a copy of a letter from Sir Rupert Hart-Davis, a famous publisher, to Valerie Eliot soon after T. S. Eliot's death in 1965. It offers a rare glimpse into the bust's life in the Eliot household. Writing soon after what would have been Eliot's 80th birthday, Hart-Davis says:

'I feel I must send you a word of love and remembrance. I can recall every moment of that happy occasion ten years ago, when I opened the champagne all over the Epstein bust, Epstein made a little speech, and Tom blew out the candles on the cake, and said "This is the happiest birthday I've ever had."'

Today, Eliot College has several other portraits of the poet. An oil painting by Patrick Heron hangs in the staff common room. Heron executed a number of portraits of Eliot, but this is the only one painted from life. It was paid for by a donation by the Linbury Trust, and is worth over £200,000. The display in the room also includes a number of photographs of T. S. Eliot throughout his life, donated by Professor Ray Pahl, and one of Valerie Eliot's favourite photographic portraits of her husband, taken by Angus McBean.

Above Portrait of T. S. Eliot by Patrick Heron (1948-50)

appears towards the centre of the painting. The modern imagery includes a bank manager wearing a Mackintosh and arranging a loan in front of a NatWest caravan. Eliot College Master Stephen Burke explains, 'As the story goes, the NatWest bank got burned down during the war, and for a while they were operating from caravans'. It was given to the university in the 1980s, when the Canterbury branch of NatWest was being refurbished.

On the other side of the hall is a triptych by Oliver Postgate, *A Canterbury Chronicle*, depicting the history of Kent. This was paid for by a £6,000 donation from Major Stanley Holland and his wife Marjorie. Major Holland was very involved with the first college: 'the Major and his wife had no children, and the students became surrogate ones instead,' says Stephen Burke. Postgate lives in the nearby village of Blean, and is famous for creating much-loved children's TV programmes including *Bagpuss* and *The Clangers*.

On leaving Eliot College, we walk past several framed posters, which tell the story of the life and times of T. S. Eliot. These were a gift from a British Council exhibition about the author. Returning down the Eliot causeway and turning left past the Marlowe Building, we come to the Jarman Building, home to the School of Art.

Above *Autumn* by Wenzel Hollar (1641). From the Kent Print collection, catalogue no. UKPC.2013.028

Opposite page *Hymn* sculpture by Stephen Cox (1990)

Below *Drawings Towards 'Hymn'* by Stephen Cox (1992)

NEXT STOP: THE JARMAN BUILDING

The Jarman Building is an award-winning Arts building named after film-maker and artist Derek Jarman, who used to live in Dungeness, Kent. It houses Studio 3, an exhibition space that displays work from cutting-edge artists as well as historical pieces. Since it opened in 2010, Studio 3 has received in-kind support and art loans from over 150 different art galleries, dealerships and artists themselves.

In the staff common room hangs the oil painting *Mysterious Landscape* (2010) by Frederick Cuming RA. The oil painting was donated by Cuming, who received an honorary doctorate from the university in 2004. It depicts a T-shaped sculpture not dissimilar to Stephen Cox's work *Hymn*, described below, which is located near to Keynes College on the Canterbury Campus. The sculpture is set within a Dungeness landscape, and inspired by the 'Angel of the South', a navigation sign that was put up in Dungeness to help fishermen find their way across the channel prior to modern navigational technologies. Cuming's contribution to the university was unveiled in March 2012.

Also housed in the Jarman building is the Kent Print Collection. Founded in 2005 by Dr Ben Thomas, Lecturer in History and Philosophy of Art, the collection operates under the rule that only students taking an undergraduate module on 'Print Collecting and Curating' may buy works for the collection. The students on the course are set a task of writing an exhibition bid, suggesting new acquisitions and potential loans for the exhibition. The winning exhibition proposal is then carried forward, and the students put on the exhibition at the end of the course.

All other items in the collection are obtained by donation or are on permanent loan. Several hundred prints from the collection were donated by Mr P. Y. Chin, of the art dealership Chinfineart.

The collection includes: two 16th-century prints by John Chown; copies of the work of major printmakers of the Renaissance; an etching by Ana Maria Pacheco depicting a scene reminiscent of Chaucer's Canterbury Tales; and three etchings by Harry Ecclestone, the designer of British banknotes from 1958-1983.

NEXT STOP: *HYMN*

Coming out of the Jarman Building and turning right brings us to a road that forms the main thoroughfare and bus route through the campus. To mark the University of Kent's silver jubilee in 1990, a large sculpture was commissioned and placed on the grass near University Road and the Keynes bus stop, so that students, staff and visitors would see it as they passed. The result was *Hymn,* an Indian granite sculpture by Stephen Cox. Stephen Bann, Professor of Art, secured funding to commission the work from the Henry Moore Foundation. The late Alan Wyndham Green of Godinton, near Ashford, also contributed – his Trust is mentioned on the plaque beside the sculpture.

Art critic Richard Cork describes the sculpture as seeming 'to have taken root in the surroundings',[17] much as the University of Kent's campus as a whole has rooted itself within its patch of Kent countryside. Inside Keynes College itself, visitors can see a number of Cox's preparatory studies for *Hymn*. These were presented to the College by Cox, and were originally exhibited in a special exhibition, *Drawings Towards 'Hymn'*, in 1992.

NEXT STOP: *HUELLA HUMANA*

Continuing out of Keynes College and back towards the Stacey Building, we come across a striking sculpture of a female nude within a DNA helix. This work, *Huella Humana* ('human fingerprint'), was created to honour the work of Dr Louise H. Naylor, a Senior Lecturer in Biochemistry at the university who worked on left-handed Z-DNA for her PhD thesis. She received a grant from the Royal Society and the British Association Millennium Awards to construct a bronze sculpture representing the development of DNA and genetic research over the 20th century. The sculpture was produced in collaboration with local artist Asuncion Bassas-Mujtaba. The sculpture, which was unveiled in 1999, is notably left-handed, and features the handprint of Naylor's daughter Kirsty.

Right *Huella Humana* sculpture by Asuncion Bassas-Mujtaba (1999)

We now pass under the Stacey Building, named after the founding Director of Biosciences, Professor Ken Stacey, who died in 2010. The Biosciences department has its own charitable fund, The Stacey Fund, which enables students from low-income families to gain laboratory experience and improve their employment prospects. Professor Stacey's family have also donated generously to the School of Biosciences, and fund a yearly symposium in his name.

The school also holds the Annual Wain Medal lecture series, funded by an endowment from the family of Professor Louis Wain, a former Professor of Chemistry in the School. The medal is awarded to a biochemistry scientist every year.

NEXT STOP: KENT SPORT

On the other side of the Stacey building is the Sports Building. Sport has a strong association with philanthropy at Kent. The 'Project 100' fundraising initiative, launched as part of the university's 50th anniversary celebrations, hopes to build upon 50 years of sports successes by raising money to support the next 50 years. The idea is to garner small amounts of support from the large number of people who use the sports facilities. 'If 1,000 people give £20 a year, that's £20,000 a year,' says Graham Holmes, the current Director of Sport. 'However many commit to giving a small sum, we will build on that year on year.'

Nowhere on campus is 'everyday philanthropy' more in evidence than the Sports Building. Instead of philanthropy being represented by dramatic statues, sculptures or plaques, the gifts that contribute to Kent Sport are in daily use by many hundreds of students and staff. The first sports hall and squash courts were built back in 1968. By 1971, a campaign had already begun to build new changing rooms near the grass pitches: the keen sportsmen and women of the 1970s had to make do with a wooden hut next to the cricket pitch.

PROJECT

Above Kent Sport

A group of donors known as the 'Friends of the Sports Hall' helped pay for a secondary sports hall in the complex.[18] Yet the most significant donation to Kent Sport came many years later. In 2005, Kent Sport had applied to the Football Foundation (the largest UK sports charity, funded by the Premier League and the Football Association) for a grant towards a new Sports Pavilion and football pitches. The bid was unsuccessful. Two years later, Graham Holmes rewrote the application. By this point, two new artificial pitches had already been built, due to a requirement from Sport England (the non-departmental government body that funds sport development) to replace old pitches. The original bid had claimed enhancing the facilities would increase the number of people playing football, but the reworked bid changed the argument:

> 'What we said was "we have got the numbers, but we now need to service them: we need to give them somewhere to change". We also said, "this is a more iconic facility than one you might get somewhere else... It's a focal point. So when people come to play football, it has that wow factor."' —Graham Holmes

The Football Foundation donated a sum of nearly £1 million for the refurbishment of the Sports Centre in 2007. The work was completed in October 2009, when the new Sports Pavilion opened near Parkwood student accommodation, on the far west side of campus.

LAST STOP: SYNAPSE-SOLEIL

As you stand outside the Sports Building, ahead and to your left is yet another eye-catching sculpture. It sits atop a pedestal outside the Jennison Building, a pedestal that lay bare for almost 50 years. Roger Jennison, the first Professor of Electronics, was also an amateur artist, and placed the plinth in its present position with a view to supporting a statue which he himself proposed to make. The statue was to feature three prominent scientists – Isaac Newton, Max Planck and Albert Einstein – plus a fourth figure, kneeling at their feet inserting a brick into the foundations. Due to some concerns about who would be chosen as inspiration for the fourth statue, his proposal was turned down.[19]

However, the plinth remained. In 2014, the School of Engineering and Digital Arts (EDA), in association with Creative Campus, launched a competition for staff and students to create a design for a permanent sculpture that would best reflect the School's reputation and vision, to be placed on the plinth.

Synapse-Soleil is the work of Michael Green and Sam Frewer, PhD students at the School of Engineering and Digital Arts based in the Jennison Building. The work was partly funded by John Washington, a university benefactor who supports many different campus initiatives – including the Ingenuity Fund, which funds postgraduate students displaying public-mindedness and entrepreneurial spirit in their studies.

This short tour demonstrates how philanthropy has become embedded into the campus over time. It has shown how even the smallest donations have come to shape the landscape at the University of Kent. Yet as we will see, even the existence of the university in the first place was dependent upon philanthropic gifts.

Left *Synapse-Soleil* sculpture, designed by Michael Green and Sam Frewer, constructed by Michael Hart

3
INCEPTION
THE BIRTH OF A UNIVERSITY

T he city of Canterbury began life as a small Iron Age settlement, growing in size when it was taken over and rebuilt by the Romans in the 1st century AD. This little town in Kent came to prominence through the establishment of St Augustine's monastery just outside of the old Roman city walls. In 603, Canterbury became the seat of the country's first Archbishop.

The ecclesiastic presence in Canterbury has remained strong up to the present day. As a consequence, many philanthropic institutions exist in the town centre, including schools, hospitals set up to care for the sick and impoverished, and a number of almshouses. The oldest charity in the country, the King's School, founded in 597, continues to operate in Canterbury. In a town with such a rich history of charitable giving, philanthropy has been a natural catalyst for progress and change.

Although it was state funding that brought it into being, the University of Kent was also founded on local support and philanthropic gifts. The new university would not have been built in Canterbury at all had it not been for the support of local councils and local education bodies, who promised land, administrative support, and help in kind when the project was still just an idea. This chapter uses documents from the university's archives to construct the story of how philanthropy spurred this particular 1960s university into being.

In May 1959, the Kent Further Education Planning Committee – a body of academics, local headteachers, college directors and others involved in education charged with overseeing the proposal – began to investigate the idea of having a university in Kent.

As with all the new universities, many of the set-up costs had to be met locally: national funding only started to flow once the teaching started. Furthermore, money from the University Grants Committee (UGC) was not supposed to be used for building student residences or a ceremonial hall, both central to Kent's vision of the new university as a scholarly community.

Fundraising began in 1960. Lord Cornwallis, Lord Lieutenant of Kent and former chairman of Kent County Council, was elected as the first chairman of 'The Sponsors of a University of Kent'. This collection of distinguished Kentish residents developed from the Education Planning Committee, which had become too large to deal with the everyday business of setting up a university. The Sponsors were not necessarily financial benefactors: rather, they wished to support the project through giving their time, possibly as eventual governors, and opening their address books for fundraising purposes.

Fundraising was directed at four sources of potential funds: local authorities, local businesses, local individuals of standing – 'the great and the good' of Kent – and finally, the general public. Local authorities were already more or less on board, the county council in particular needing little convincing of the merits of a project that would bring jobs and prestige to Kent.

LOCATION OF THE UNIVERSITY

At this early stage, the location of the new university was not fixed and there was no shortage of suggestions from local government bodies across the county, all eager to see the new institution built on their patch (see Table 1).

> " The people of Kent had long wanted a university of their own, and one which would be worthy of the county; there was now great hope that this would come to fruition, provided they helped towards its realisation.'
>
> Lord Cornwallis, June 1965

The University Grants Committee

The University Grants Committee (UGC) was a government advisory body first given status in 1919. Its role was to address the distribution of public money to universities, which was more pressing than ever after World War II, during which many university buildings had been reappropriated or damaged.

Above Proposal for a
University in Thanet, 1959

**Table 1: Proposed
University Sites,
1959–61**

Ashford: Eastwell Park;
Hothfield
Canterbury: Rough
Common; Bourne Park;
Nackington
Dover: Castle Heights
Folkestone-Hythe: Capel-
le-Ferne; Small Arms School;
Beachborough
Thanet: Palm Bay,
Kingsgate; Ramsgate Airport

Thanet was an early front-runner, thanks to the enthusiastic proposal put forward by Thanet Technical College, a further education institution in Broadstairs. The 'University of Thanet' was envisaged as occupying a small 90-acre site that encompassed Ramsgate Airport in East Kent.

The Education Planning Committee was not convinced. In its view, the university would require a 120–150 acre site; the Thanet site was also unsuitable in that it would mean the loss of prime agricultural land. Despite press reports in August 1959 appearing to confirm Thanet as the preferred site (purportedly leaked by a member of Thanet's local education committee), the Committee postponed its decision. In April 1960 an alternative location emerged. Canterbury City Council offered a piece of land large enough to satisfy the Committee: 267 acres of hillside north of the old suburb of St Dunstan's. But another six months of discussion ensued before a final decision on the location of the new university was made.

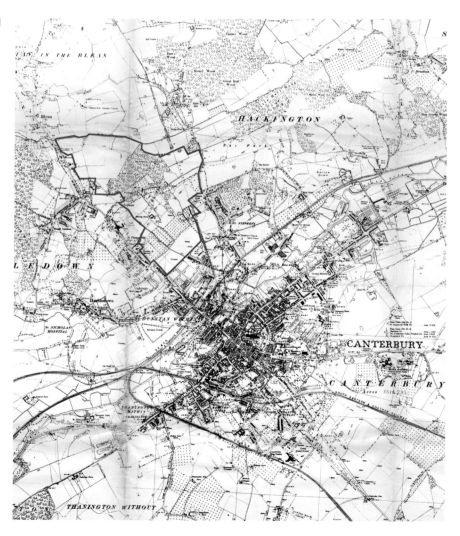

Right Map of Canterbury
showing original outline for
the university site, drawn in
marker pen in 1960

FIRST FUNDRAISING EFFORTS: COURTING INDUSTRIAL SUPPORT

The first formal fundraising effort targeted local industry and commerce. The Education Planning Committee compiled a list of 'Firms of Standing and Substance' in Kent, which were then to be tentatively approached to see if they might offer financial support to a new higher education institution in the county. At that time, Kent's industries included engineering, cement manufacture, paper-making, mining, and agriculture. The 'selling point' was that a local university would create a local supply of graduates trained in areas that complemented their businesses.

A cordial message was sent out to a select few business owners in Kent, inviting them to a luncheon hosted by one of the Sponsors, Lord Bossom. The express aim of the luncheon was 'to persuade them to offer substantial financial support to our new university'.

Even before Lord Bossom's lunch had taken place, Pfizer Ltd offered to give the new university £50,000 – equivalent to over £800,000 today. The Sponsors used this generous donation as a model to persuade other firms to give. Pfizer's pledge demonstrated, firstly, that the new university was deemed to be a sound investment; and secondly, that the local business community should have an interest in making the new institution a success. The main argument made by those seeking philanthropic support was that local businesses were bound to benefit from the university's presence, but only if they joined the club of supporters.

During the fundraising lunch, various parties, including future benefactors, expressed an interest in the university being sited at Canterbury. At this stage, the site was not finally fixed, although the Sponsors had recommended Canterbury to the UGC. The managing director of BP's Isle of Grain refinery was particularly pleased at the Canterbury location; he also expressed his company's particular interest in science graduates.

£2 million was required from the outset, to enable the new university to provide residential places on campus for 3,000 students by 1970, as well as to

Below left Invitation from Lord Bossom to Commander D. S. E. Thompson, Chairman of Kent Education Committee

Below right BP Advert, *Kent Messenger* Supplement, 15 October 1975

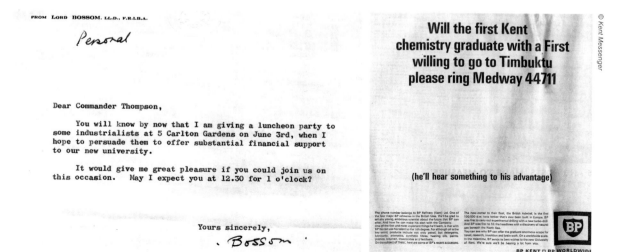

FROM LORD BOSSOM. LL.D., F.R.I.B.A.

Personal

Dear Commander Thompson,

You will know by now that I am giving a luncheon party to some industrialists at 5 Carlton Gardens on June 3rd, when I hope to persuade them to offer substantial financial support to our new university.

It would give me great pleasure if you could join us on this occasion. May I expect you at 12.30 for 1 o'clock?

Yours sincerely,

. Bossom .

Will the first Kent chemistry graduate with a First willing to go to Timbuktu please ring Medway 44711

(he'll hear something to his advantage)

© Kent Messenger

BP KENT □ BP WORLDWIDE

PFIZER LTD

On 25 May 1960, Pfizer Ltd pledged a donation of £50,000 – equivalent to over £800,000 in today's money. This was the first and largest of the early corporate donations to the new university. An American pharmaceutical company, Pfizer began operations in the UK in the early 1950s, establishing a vast 80-acre site in Sandwich in 1954. The company's donation was warmly received, not least as a model to encourage other businesses to give.

Pfizer Ltd remains one of the most significant donors to the University of Kent, despite significantly scaling back its presence in Sandwich in 2010. The firm has funded a Chair in Medical Statistics for eight years, and provided £500,000 to establish a head of the School of Pharmacy at Kent's Medway campus, which opened in 2004. The company donated money to establish a library for the Kent Institute of Medicine and Health Services (KIMHS), sponsored a chemistry lab, and an art gallery in Keynes College, and employees at Pfizer occasionally guest lectured on undergraduate courses.

The relationship between the firm and university is perhaps best demonstrated by the decision by Kent Innovation and Enterprise (KIE), the university's dedicated business support department, to move some of their services to Discovery Park, the former Pfizer site in Sandwich, now an international hub of biotechnology, life sciences, medical research and business. Pfizer still retain a presence at the site, and together with KIE will help foster future collaborations between industry, students and academics.

The original donation from Pfizer established a pattern of knowledge transfer and industry partnerships which has an enduring legacy at the University of Kent.

> "We believe in the future! – a future which can only be built if there is an adequate proportion of scientific and other university-trained people in our community.
>
> Philip V. Colebrook, Managing Director of Pfizer, 30 May 1960

Below Discovery Park, formerly the Pfizer site at Sandwich

© Discovery Park

construct teaching buildings. The UGC required at least 10% of this figure to come from voluntary sources, along with a continued contribution to maintenance. At the end of the 1960 appeal luncheon, Lord Bossom stated that the university hoped to receive £200,000 from local authorities, and that, ideally, those present at the lunch would collectively donate £300,000, thus achieving a total of £500,000. Although several companies pledged donations in the months that followed, the figures fell far short of the target. BP gave £25,000, as did Associated Portland Cement Manufacturers and Unilever Ltd.

Some donations were made as preliminary pledges, with an offer of further funds dependent on the university developing teaching or research in their areas of interest. For example, A. E. Reed and Co., a paper manufacturer, pledged £20,000 on top of an initial £10,000, but only if the university opened an engineering department. Chemical company Albright & Wilson Ltd requested that its gift be used directly to fund science, specifically Chemistry, and also asked that the firm 'or some part of it will be able to take a continuing interest in the affairs of the particular department it is aimed to support'.

The Wellcome Foundation was another donor that, although not a profit-making company, had an interest in donating to the new university in Kent. Their nearby laboratories, chemical works and research centres in Beckenham, Dartford and Frant were crying out for young graduates and research that furthered their vision.

The practice of tying philanthropic donations to specific practical outcomes is nothing new. Tudor merchants and Georgian ship-owners supported charity schools in part to improve skills in book-keeping and navigation. In the 1960s, enthusiasm for 'the white heat of technology' led governments of all persuasions to encourage university ties with industry: collaborations would justify the initial state investment, and help boost Britain's economy. As we will see in later chapters, donations from industry continue to generate outcomes that benefit both donor and recipient.

Above Development and advancement of technology was integral to the early university

Left Wellcome Advert, *Kent Messenger* Supplement, 15 October 1975.

© Kent Messenger

The Wellcome Foundation salutes the University of Kent

At Beckenham in Kent, the Wellcome Research Laboratories and the Wellcome Laboratories of Tropical Medicine carry out diverse research activities in order to combat all types of disease, both animal and human.

At Dartford, in Kent, the Wellcome Chemical Works is the main production and distribution centre of the Wellcome Foundation in Britain and a wide range of preparations is produced for the home markets and for export.

Set in the farming country on the Kent/Sussex border, the Wellcome Veterinary Research Station, Frant, studies infection and dietary problems in animals, in natural conditions.

The Wellcome Foundation Limited is a private company. Its shares are owned by the Wellcome Trust which applies all profits distributed as dividend for the support of medical and allied research throughout the world.

BURROUGHS WELLCOME & CO. (The Wellcome Foundation Ltd.) LONDON

Above Cartoon of Geoffrey Templeman by *inCant* artist 'Ted' (E. P. G. Harrison), *inCant*, 1 February 1966

The level of donations produced by the 1960 luncheon was disappointing. But, with hindsight, the early fundraising efforts were hampered by two main factors. Kent was relatively lacking in local industry that was able and likely to support a new university, compared to the West Midlands or the North. Of the industries present in the area, agriculture was the largest – yet the university did not plan to develop a faculty of agriculture.

The second factor was, perhaps, more avoidable. This was the 1962 decision by the Interim Committee, which had taken charge of fundraising efforts, not to use professional fundraisers. The Sponsors seem to have been split on the matter but eventually opted to handle fundraising themselves, a decision partly influenced by Geoffrey Templeman, the university's future first Vice-Chancellor, who had come to Kent from the University of Birmingham, where he had been Registrar since 1955. During his time in the Midlands he had been impressed by the industrialist Lord Rootes, whose efforts on behalf of the new University of Warwick were credited with steering its successful £4 million fundraising campaign.[20] Rootes had operated through personal connections and Templeman believed that 'the Rootes method' was all that was needed. '[If] a highly placed and influential person is chairman of the Appeal Committee,' he said, 'then I think the mechanics of the business will take care of themselves.'[21]

By 1963, the plans for the new university were well underway. A 10-year plan was discussed during an appeal subcommittee meeting, which calculated a need for £3 million to meet the planned growth up to 1973. This included £2 million for 'essential student accommodation'; £750,000 for 'other capital needs' which included the university library and the funding of chairs, scholarships, grants and research; and £250,000 for a ceremonial hall. Lord Cornwallis confided in a letter to Dr John Haynes, County Education Officer and Secretary to the Sponsors, that 'York and Norwich have both appealed for £1,500,000 and I am that certain that we cannot do with less'.

The original appeal goal was £2 million from private sources. However, faith in the campaign faltered from the outset. By March 1964, the projected appeal goal was lowered to £1,500,000, to take account of any potential short-fall from industry donations. By October 1964, the figure had dropped again: Sir Cecil Syers, Head of the Appeal Committee, remarked that it was 'unrealistic to hope for more than, at most, £1,250,000'.[22]

Publicly, however, the university continued to keep up appearances, maintaining the £2 million target throughout. In December 1964, a working committee was formed and a public appeal began to take shape. The aim was not just to reach the public in Kent, but also potential donors in the rest of the UK. The message was clear: government funds were insufficient to cover the cost of residences for the number of students the new university hoped to attract, even though by 1964 the UGC had relented on its initial restrictions, and permitted the grant to be used for building Eliot College, the university's first residential block.

The appeal message was to be heavily promoted through local press and TV, leafleting and personal canvassing. In addition, mayors of Borough Councils, and chairmen of District Councils, would 'undertake responsibility in their own areas for effective follow-up of the Public Appeal, setting up for this purpose small committees of active people who would undertake personal canvassing of both individuals and business firms'.[23] Sponsors were urged to make personal approaches, with Sir Cecil Syers observing that: 'The tongue is more potent than the pen.'

For the local county, a target was set of £500,000: roughly six shillings per Kent resident.

SECOND STAGE OF FUNDRAISING EFFORTS: THE PUBLIC APPEAL

In May 1965, press, local and county council representatives, and Sponsors attended a press conference to announce the official launch of the public appeal on Friday 11 June 1965. Lord Cornwallis's speech on the occasion underlined that local pride was at stake:

> *'The people of Kent had long wanted a University of their own, and one which would be worthy of the County; there was now great hope that this would come to fruition, provided they helped towards its realisation.*
>
> *'Dr Johnson had observed that when a man knows he is to be hanged in a fortnight, it concentrates his thoughts wonderfully. That same spirit of urgency must be applied to the building of the University and its Appeal, if it was to achieve the success which it must'.*[24]

The appeal began to spread the message beyond the 'great and the good' to the wider population. There was support from the local press, including direct appeals in the *Kent Messenger* and *Kentish Gazette*, as well as a 30-minute documentary broadcast on *Southern TV* on 13 July 1965. The University Foundation Fund was technically regarded as a charity, and therefore was able to obtain free TV coverage as an appeal or 'good cause' under the Independent Television Authority's licence.

Additionally, the Appeal committee distributed 90,000 leaflets, and 6,000 personally-addressed letters to 'larger industrial companies, larger professional firms and selected wealthy individuals',[25] signed by Lord Cornwallis.

The first intake of students arrived in October 1965. Nicknamed the 'First 500' after the Marlowe Theatre play that was put on to raise money for the Foundation Fund Appeal (the actual number of students was closer to 450), the group went about settling in to their college and attending lectures in a sea of mud due to incomplete building work.

Despite a concerted effort, the response continued to fall below expectations and the campaign target was further revised downwards to £1 million in early 1966. This sum would cover the cost of the first three colleges, but fail to pay for the rest of the plans, which included at least two more colleges, a library building and a central multipurpose hall.

The first appeal struggled for a number of reasons. One problem was the reorganisation of local government boundaries in 1965, when the affluent areas in Bromley and Bexley left Kent to become London boroughs, thus ending any possibility of fundraising for county causes in those parts. A further problem was caused by the timing of the death of Sir Winston Churchill in early 1965, as the subsequent public appeal in his memory attracted great support in Kent and left many local borough councils reluctant to take on any

© Kentish Gazette

Above Geoffrey Templeman, Vice-Chancellor, explains why the university needs philanthropic money. *Kentish Gazette*, 1 October 1965

"

There's one thing you must be if you want to start a university... A fanatic.

Announcer, University of Kent at Canterbury Feature by *Southern Television*, aired 13 July 1965

© Kent Messenger

MARLOWE THEATRE,
CANTERBURY
SUNDAY, NOVEMBER 14 at 8 p.m.

'THE FIRST 500'

A LIGHT-HEARTED ANTHOLOGY BEING BY WAY
OF A WELCOME TO THE NEW UNIVERSITY OF KENT
AT CANTERBURY

❄

ARRANGED BY BARRY CAMPBELL

❄

Proceeds from all tickets sold
to the University Appeal Fund

❄

Sponsored by the Kent Messenger

Above The Marlowe
Theatre's 'First 500' play,
the proceeds of which went
to the Appeal Fund

Right Lord Cornwallis's
letter, asking for donations
to the Appeal Fund

further fundraising duties. It is unclear why many nearby boroughs did not manage to offer support, despite having influential donors living within their boundaries; they may have felt their ratepayers were already contributing to the new university through the county rates.

Also hampering the progress of the appeal was unfortunate economic timing. The postponement of the public appeal until after the Budget was announced in 1965 was an error; this was the year the Finance Act was brought in, requiring businesses to pay corporation tax (prior to this point they had only paid income tax on profits). This would have hit many companies hard, discouraging philanthropy from industry.

CHANCELLOR
Her Royal Highness Princess Marina, Duchess of Kent
PRO CHANCELLOR
The Right Honourable, Lord Cornwallis, K.B.E.,M.C.
VICE CHANCELLOR
Geoffrey Templeman, M.A., Ph.D., F.S.A
DEPUTY PRO CHANCELLOR
Sir George Allen, C.B.E., B.Ch., M.D.

UNIVERSITY OF KENT AT CANTERBURY
WESTGATE HOUSE, CANTERBURY · TELEPHONE 66191

June, 1965.

　　As Lord Lieutenant of the County and Pro-Chancellor of the University I ask my Kent friends to give - and give generously - to the Appeal Fund of this, our own, University. Its foundation is the greatest event that has taken place in the County in our lifetime, the greatest - it may be - for many centuries. Let us all help to make this University great and famous, a proud member of the family of British Universities, worthy in every way of the long history and traditions of our County and our ancient Cathedral City.

　　Please find time to read the booklet, which tells you what we plan and what we need; do not lay it aside without resolving to give something. Every contribution, large or small, will be welcome and is vital if this splendid project is to be realised.

Cornwallis –

Her Majesty's Lieutenant of Kent
Pro-Chancellor of the University.

As a result of these unpredictable factors and general low levels of enthusiasm, by January 1966, with the students already one term into their degree at the new university, the public portion of the appeal had only raised a total of £81,000 – not an insignificant figure, but £450,000 less than the sum the fundraising committee had hoped for from the Kent population. By June 1966, the whole appeal (both the early private phase and the public appeal) had raised only £563,000.[26, 27]

The early history of philanthropy at Kent provided many potential lessons for future fundraising. Yet it would be two decades before a permanent fundraising expertise was established on campus, as part of preparations for the Silver Anniversary in 1988, when a Development Department was finally created. Since this time, there has been some successful fundraising efforts, strong partnerships, lasting legacies and potential avenues for future fundraising that are yet to be explored. However, the note of caution in this tale of the Foundation Fund Appeal is tangible. The historical context, the nature of local industry, and the proficiency of professionals in the fundraising field were not heeded. The following chapters will show how Kent continued to learn from the experience.

4
EXCELLENCE
BUILDING A DISTINCTIVE UNIVERSITY

The pursuit of academic excellence is a core value of every leading Higher Education Institution, including the University of Kent. The pursuit of excellence is part of the university's institutional plan, to build 'our inspiring and distinctive education that prepares our students to make a positive contribution to help shape a better world'. The Research Excellence Framework (REF), the national assessment of universities' scholarly activity, ranked Kent 17th in the UK for research intensity in December 2014, and the university was judged to have world-leading research in all the subjects submitted for assessment.

Philanthropy has always played a role in facilitating these achievements. From the very start, gifts were offered for academic chairs, research fellowships and scholarships. The Astor Foundation gave one of the first gifts toward promoting excellence at Kent, before the buildings were even finished in mid-1965 – £5,250 to further the musical offerings on campus. Alan Laing, the first Director of Music, was able to use the money to build the music library, offer scholarships and purchase instruments for students, put on recitals and even pay for the orchestra costs for various musical theatre pieces, including full-scale operas.

Since then, philanthropic gifts have continued to contribute to the university's reputation for excellence. This chapter reflects on some of the philanthropic activity that helps students, encourages scholarship, and promotes the distinctive nature of excellence at the University of Kent. Many gifts aim to generate excellence in academic research and teaching; others seek to relieve hardship for capable students in financial difficulties.

SUPPORTING STUDENT EXCELLENCE

Academic excellence is located within human beings – their ingenuity, curiosity and achievement. Without the people to do the thinking, talking and learning, universities would fail. Funding individuals through scholarships has been a feature of the University of Kent since the earliest days and the institution now boasts a long history of philanthropic support for capable students.

The university is lucky to receive funding towards student scholarships in many different fields – not only academic, but also in sport, music and the creative arts. Many scholarships owe their existence to individual donors; others are established in memory of a former student or member of staff. Ninety different philanthropic scholarships and awards are given to deserving students every year. There is something timeless and moving about the practice of individuals helping other individuals across the generations.

One of the earliest scholarship funds received by the University of Kent was the Dora Harvey Memorial Scholarship, given in memory of local woman Dora Harvey to support female students pursuing a PhD in the Social Sciences. It was set up in October 1967, and supports students to this day. Since then, countless scholarships have been funded, and almost every Department has its own. This chapter will offer a selection of illuminating examples.

Below A 'First 500' reunion

GENERATION TO GENERATION SCHOLARSHIPS

The First 500 Group is made up of students from the university's first cohort of students, who arrived in 1965. The Group recently set up the First 500 Fund, in honour of the university's 50th anniversary. This has raised £43,000 to date and aims to establish a First 500 Bursary, which will allow future students to enjoy the same opportunities that the Group's members benefited from 50 years ago. Staff have been involved in similar initiatives: the Former Staff Association was established in 2008 and has supported many campus causes, including the Colyer-Fergusson Music Building described in Chapter 2.

Some donors give to help the students of a specific college with which they were associated. The Rutherford Master's Fund was established by Dr Alan Hearne, a former Rutherford student and Honorary Doctor of Science at Kent. In his oration for Dr Hearne, Professor Simon Thompson described how 'Alan wouldn't have come to Kent without a grant – and in his final year he was kept going by a Master's loan of £50; an act of generosity which he hasn't forgotten'. Dr Hearne subsequently donated a sum of £25,000 to help Rutherford students whose financial hardship may prevent them from completing their degree course.

Not only former students contribute toward future generations. A donation of £55,000 was made to the university in 2012 from the estate of Barbara Harris, the first Bursar of Eliot College. This funded the Barbara Harris Scholarship, which provides two £1,000 bursaries a year for Business, Accounting and Finance undergraduates. It also funded the Eliot Master's Fund which, like the Rutherford Master's Fund, helps students who are in a position of hardship.

MEMORIAL SCHOLARSHIPS

The Christine and Ian Bolt Scholarship was established by Ian Bolt in 2005 in memory of his wife Christine, who was Professor of American History and Pro Vice-Chancellor at the University of Kent. When Ian passed away in 2008, he left a legacy that would continue to support the scholarship for years to come. The scholarship provides £10,000 for a postgraduate student to carry out research in the United States. Previous work supported by the scholarship includes the legacy of US President John F. Kennedy, the poetry of James Joyce, and psychopathology in primates.

This scholarship, like many others at Kent, supports partnerships with overseas institutions as well as encouraging research excellence in new subject areas. The gift also funds an annual Bolt Lecture in the Centre for American Studies.

Below Michael Mills, Christine and Ian Bolt Scholar 2014–15

'Thanks to the funding for my doctoral research provided by the Christine and Ian Bolt Scholarship, I was able to gain unprecedented access in the contemporary American prepping scene (a contemporary label for American survivalist activities). The funding was used to travel to America and meet dozens of preppers face-to-face, interview them, and see in intimate settings what they do and why – allowing empirical data to be gained that has, as of yet, not emerged in relation to a widespread lifestyle about which not much is known.

'I believe this is a good example of how philanthropic funding – particularly that devoted to supporting cutting-edge research, as is the case with the Ian and Christine Bolt Scholarship – can be used positively, and how its independence allows the restrictive criteria of other funding bodies to be circumnavigated. This is clearly to the benefit of valuable and expansive social research.'—Michael Mills, PhD student and recipient of the Christine and Ian Bolt Scholarship, 2014–15.

Many other memorial scholarships have been funded in memory of staff, students and friends of the university. Numerous benefactors also fund the esteemed Music and Sports Scholarships programmes to enable talented musicians and sportspeople to continue these extra-curricula activities, and not miss out on a full university education.

MUSIC SCHOLARSHIPS

In 2014, generous donations supported 32 music scholarships, worth between £1,000 and £2,000 each, enabling the scholars to continue their studies whilst practising and performing music in the university's new Colyer-Fergusson music building.

One such donation led to the Richard Scase Big Band Fund, which allows students to take music lessons, attend workshops, and buy instruments. As the name suggests, the donor has a special interest in preserving the heritage of Big Band music. Richard Scase, who is Emeritus Professor of Sociology and Organisational Behaviour at Kent, comments, 'I enjoy all kinds of music – classical, opera, world – but have a particular penchant for Sinatra-style and Big Band. I am keen for young musicians and their audiences to learn and appreciate the heritage of all music forms and discover where their own passion lies.'

Below Joe Prescott playing a solo with the University of Kent Big Band

SPORTS SCHOLARSHIPS

Similar scholarships promote excellence in sport. Kent County Cricket Club (KCCC) funds a scholarship for promising young cricketers in the county, in partnership with the university. As a sports scholar, a student receives high-level cricket tuition from KCCC, alongside support from Kent Sport. This arrangement enables the club to train the best young cricketers whilst they study locally. The fund was established as a legacy by two local brothers, J & K Huntley.

A number of hockey scholarships are offered in partnership with the Canterbury Ladies' and Canterbury Men's, Holcombe, Old Bordenians, and Maidstone hockey clubs. The recipient receives money towards their studies, and in return will play for the university and the local clubs' teams. Similarly, Canterbury Rugby Club offers funding towards a rugby scholar on the university's rugby team. Kent Sport also offers the David James Boxing Scholarship, set up by donor John Horton in honour of his friend and boxing coach the late David James, former Director of Kent Sport. It has also set up the Mike Wilkins Football Scholarship fund, named after another former Director of Sport at Kent.

It is not only scholarships that are funding excellence at Kent Sport. Money received in partnership with the Tennis Foundation pays for a tennis development co-ordinator to work with Kent Sport in the new Sports Pavilion. The Pavilion was refurbished as the result of a philanthropic donation from the Football Foundation in 2009, and includes a new tennis centre.

THE MEDWAY STUDENT SUPPORT FUND

Working with the University of Greenwich and Canterbury Christ Church University in Medway has enabled the University of Kent to provide financial support for local students, thus widening access to higher education in a region that has a lower than average take-up of education beyond the age of 16.

This is helped by the Medway Student Support Fund, a philanthropic fund set up by an anonymous donor, which is distributed across the three different institutions to ensure the money is disbursed wherever need is greatest. In 2014, the gift of £50,000 helped make a difference to the lives of 19 students struggling with financial difficulties, and has had the added benefit of helping to strengthen the relationship between the three institutions.

'I contributed to the Medway Student Support Fund because the Universities at Medway campus provides a wonderful opportunity for people of all backgrounds to go to university and realise their potential. I wanted to help prevent the cost stopping anyone from taking up this life-changing opportunity.' —Anonymous donor

'Being awarded this bursary has awarded me financial security which I didn't previously experience. I can only describe this feeling as a positive one.' —A recipient

INTERNATIONAL EXCELLENCE

Excellence in the 21st century means working internationally. The university has a proud international identity, as exemplified by the Kent strapline – 'The UK's European University' – and its active research and teaching campuses in France, Italy, Belgium and Greece. Kent also benefits from numerous individual-donor or corporate-funded scholarships and funds with overseas associations. These range from the Lo Family Scholarship, which funds Chinese and Hong Kong students studying at the Kent Business School, as part of the Hong Kong China Portal (described below); to the Cuba Arts Experience Award, funded by John Washington to enable School of Arts postgraduates to experience the creative culture of Cuba. The Santander Scholarship supports postgraduate students from Iberian and Latin American countries. The Chancellor's Scholarship for Trinidad and Tobago (donated by former Chancellor Sir Robert Worcester) helps students from these countries to study at the University of Kent.

The university has strong philanthropic ties with countries overseas that promote and foster academic excellence in individuals, building up an invaluable network of people and skills.

> "
> I've had a lot of fun giving money away.
> —John Washington, donor

HONG KONG CHINA PORTAL

The Hong Kong China Portal is a five-year, £1 million fundraising project from 2014 to 2019 to support new scholarships, student exchange and research. Kent has a strong alumni group in Hong Kong and China, and its role in the Portal is crucial. The Hong Kong and China Portal Board is chaired by Kent alumnus and donor Dr William Lo. Sir David Akers-Jones,

Top Professor Eddy Fong, Hong Kong Alumni Association

Bottom Mengwei Tu, Hong Kong Alumni Scholar and Allcorn Box Memorial Scholar

a former member of the Hong Kong government and an honorary graduate of Kent, established the Hong Kong and China Fund, which provides a yearly bursary for two students to study or undertake a work placement in Hong Kong or mainland China. Vivian Wong, the parent of a former Kent student, also established a scholarship within the Kent Law School. Alumnus Dr Kennedy Wong was a £500,000 donor to the Kent Law Campaign. In addition to individual alumni giving, the Hong Kong China Portal has facilitated the Jackie Chan Foundation funding for postgraduate Arts students.

'As a proud alumnus I will do what I can to link the University of Kent with my part of the world.' —Professor Eddy Fong, President of the Hong Kong Alumni Association

'As an international student, I was honoured with the award from the Hong Kong Alumni Scholarship and the Allcorn Box Memorial Fund: the former was crucial in helping me to undertake the research programme; the latter award was a further encouragement in sustaining my research. It is difficult for an outsider to appreciate how fundamental financial security is in setting off on a research programme. I am among the lucky ones to have received support for the essential purpose of scholarship for its own sake. Such generosity inspires me to think of giving support in the future.' —Mengwei Tu, PhD student and recipient of the Hong Kong Alumni Scholarship and the Allcorn Box Memorial Scholarship, 2014–15

UNIVERSITY OF KENT IN AMERICA

The UKA (University of Kent in America) Scholarship was established in 2011 to help American students study in Kent. The scholarship is funded predominantly by US alumni. It also aims to raise the profile of the University of Kent in the USA, demonstrating the university's international impact in a global higher education market. It has a fundraising target of $1 million, and is managed by the University of Kent in America Board, which includes several Kent alumni and former staff.

UNIVERSITY OF KENT IN ATHENS

In 2011, the University of Kent's European presence expanded to Greece, with the launch of a Masters in Heritage Management offered in conjunction with the Athens University of Economics and Business. Support for the Masters course came from several philanthropic sources, including the A. G. Leventis Foundation, which funds conservation and restoration of monuments in South-Eastern Europe and the promotion of Hellenic education, and the Bodossaki Foundation, which aims to further education opportunities, nature conservation and medical care in Greece.

The course has also received funding for scholarships from the Stavros Niarchos Foundation, which helps students from developing countries, and the Fulbright Foundation, which funds American students studying heritage in Greece. The Heritage Management MA works with the Athens Initiative for Heritage Conservancy, headed by Dr Evangelos Kyriakidis. It offers its students the exciting opportunity to work on projects in Eleusina, a world-famous archaeological site.

INTERNATIONAL RESEARCH CENTRES

The Kent School of European Culture and Languages (SECL) is a goldmine of philanthropic donations, in part due to its close links with archaeological and heritage conservation organisations. It was thanks to SECL's international research expertise that the University of Kent in Paris and the University of Kent in Athens came about by drawing on SECL's reputation for excellence across the disciplines of European Studies, Languages, Classics, Archaeology, Heritage Management, and Creative Arts.

John Beale, a prominent university benefactor, has given large amounts of money to support scholarships for PhD students working on excavation work in Ostia, Rome's ancient port city: these are hosted by the Centre for Late Antique Archaeology. John Beale has also enabled the project to acquire the technological equipment needed for digitising the research findings.

> 'The University of Kent's excavations at Ostia port of Rome were possible thanks to the generous support of donors. At its peak, in 2010 we had 50 students and staff working in the city centre of ancient Ostia, recording the ruins, excavating Roman rubbish deposits and undertaking geophysical and laser survey. Donations from John Beale, and grants from the Leverhulme Trust, have allowed us to reconstruct and visualise the city of Ostia as experienced by St Augustine of Hippo in AD 387, as described in key passages of his Confessions.' —Dr Luke Lavan, SECL

SECL has also received gifts from Fondazione CRT, an Italian non-profit organisation, which pays for a Postdoctoral Research Fellow and two paid work placements. The latter are for students of Italian studies, providing them with work experience opportunities: either teaching English at the University of Turin, or translation and research work at Fondazione CRT's Turin headquarters.

Below Excavations and visual reconstruction of Ostia

THE UNIVERSITY LIBRARY

The central university library on the Canterbury campus is named after Geoffrey Templeman, the first Vice-Chancellor, and has been a hive of philanthropic activity and excellence since 1965. Philanthropy has flowed into and out of the library: for example, many of the library's unique special collections have been built up almost entirely through philanthropic donations, and library staff undertake *pro bono* work for Canterbury Cathedral, supporting the management and use of the Cathedral's archives.

THE FOUNDING OF THE LIBRARY

A major concern for all the new universities of the 1960s was that they were all 'woefully short'[28] of books and other knowledge resources, in comparison to other universities that had been building their collections for decades, if not centuries. Building a higher education library from scratch was a daunting challenge: the task required acquiring an appropriate book stock, and premises to adequately house books and students.

The original university library was housed a mile away from the campus, above a shop on Station Road West, near Canterbury's West Gate. No provision was available for a library building until October 1964, when growth of the book stock prompted expansion to a hut on campus at Beverley Farm. This too was soon full, and the library colonised some additional spaces in Eliot College and the Physical Sciences building.[29]

By this point, the library was stretched across four different sites. In sheer desperation, and with students already wasting many hours trekking back and forth between campus and library, Geoffrey Templeman appealed to the UGC for £70,000 to house the library temporarily until funding for a permanent building could be found. This was approved, and temporary housing for the library was built on campus in August 1966. It is now the Estates Department building.

Right The early Templeman library

Below The original library on Station Road West

The quantity of books donated to the university library in those early years was quite remarkable. The first librarian was G. S. Darlow. Darlow's first report in January 1964 noted that over 3,000 books had been received. An early appeal was made through the *Kent Messenger*, generating over 12,000 volumes by the arrival of the first intake of students in 1965. By 1970, the total of donated books had risen to a formidable 36,638 – one fifth of the entire library collection.[30]

> *'The Librarian will welcome all gifts of books, large or small, old or new. The only test, as I said before, and it is an important one, is that they should be books appropriate to the needs of a university library.'* —Vice-Chancellor's Second Report, 1967.[31]

The records of the university library show a great variety of donors in those early days. The chief sources of gifts were the Country Landowners Association, whose Secretary was a University Sponsor; and local education institutions. Another donor was the head of a local Kent girls' school.[32] Many volumes came from the university's early corporate sponsors and benefactors, including Pfizer and Lord Cornwallis. Members of staff gave books: among them Dr Ray Pahl, latterly Professor of Sociology, and Professor Bryan Keith-Lucas, Professor of Government and first Master of Darwin College. Professor Bonamy Dobrée, an honorary Doctor of Letters of the University in 1968, together with his wife, Gladys, gave 100 rare books, including some priceless T. S. Eliot first editions with inscriptions to Dobrée himself.

Above A silver dish given by G. S. Darlow, commemorating his years of service to the university library, 1963–77

Left List of early philanthropic donors to the library

LIST OF DONORS, 9th November 1965 to 19th March 1966

Dr. R. E. Pahl	7 vols
Prof. Keith-Lucas	3 vols
Miss R.A. Nobbs, Ashford	28 music scores, and a run of the Music Teacher
The Navy League	The Times index, 1939–45, and 9 vols of Hansard
Mr. C. Powell-Cotton, Birchington	Catalogue of the Powell-Cotton Museum
Lincoln College, Oxford	The Journal of Philology, vol.1–35
Messrs. Furley & Page, Canterbury	1 vol.
Seismograph Service (England) Ltd	47 unbound vols of journals in the field of electrical engineering
Dr. W. G. Roe, Abingdon	2 vols
Inst. of Heraldic & Genealogical Studies	Family History (a periodical)
Pfizers Ltd	A collection of pamphlets on Western Europe
Mr. A. Archangelsky, Canterbury	4 vols
Dr C. Jolles, London	11 vols
Dr E. F. Caldin	7 vols
Miss Vera Pullinger	1 vol (Memorials of Old Kent)
Mr P. Redfern, Cranleigh	The Computer Journal, vol.1–3
East Malling Research Station	2 vols
Mr. W.H. Allyn, Athens, Ohio	5 vols
Professor Lyons	2 vols
U.S. Information Service	3 vols
Mr H.S. Kirkaldy, Cambridge	Monthly Labour Review, 1946–64 and International Labour Review, 1945–65
United Africa Company	Statistical & Economic Review, complete set
Mr E.T. Mortimore, Ashford	21 vols
Dounreay Experimental Reactor	Nuclear Science Abstracts, no 1–16
French Foreign Office	Subscription to 4 journals
British Association	97 vols

Other donors of note included: the Labour Party Library; the French Foreign Office; London Transport; the Navy League; the YMCA; United Africa Company; the American, Swiss and French Embassies; and Wye College, with which Kent would later collaborate to host courses in the Medway area. Even three of the other plate-glass universities – Lancaster, Sussex and Essex – donated small collections of books to the library.

Throughout the 1960s and into the 1970s, the library expanded across the campus, with smaller college libraries servicing the students of Eliot, Rutherford and Darwin. There were even some individual departmental libraries, for example in Cornwallis for the use of the Social Science faculty.

Right Article about the new library, *Kent Messenger* supplement, 15 October, 1965

Unpacking and shelving books in the University's temporary library.

Starting a library from scratch

N the first year of the University's active life, Library is temporarily ithout a permanent home. It the many factors that ive in recent years eatly increased the dependence of a university's embers on the Library, ade it essential to pro-

American or German standards. To supplement it, an appeal for books was made through the Kent Messenger and other newspapers, and through

prepared, limits the effectiveness of this service, but much has been done by means of documentation.

Lists

collection — the runs of scientific journals — are ruinously expensive, when they are available at all. Moreover, the prices of both past runs and current

ZI BO NA TE KI RA

LA KI TE LI LA LO

LO ZI RA GA LO TA

YELLOW WHITE MUD MOON OWL SNOW SEVEN STONES RAIN WIND MOUSE FISH HORIZONS DUSK EAST WORM TWIGS SNOW

W I N T E R

S U N S E T

S H A D O W

AN EIGHTEEN DAY ROAD WALK ACROSS SOUTHERN ENGLAND FROM LANDS END TO THE NORTH KENT COAST EARLY 1984

Left *Winter Sunset Shadow*, by Hamish Fulton (1984)

Below A pencil sketch of Harry Bloom by an unknown artist, given to the university in 1991

Besides books, the library also received works of art. The panel work by artist Hamish Fulton, *Winter Sunset Shadow*, hangs in the First Floor Reading Room. It was originally commissioned for the Canterbury Festival in 1984 and donated after the Festival was over. The library was also the recipient of generous gifts for the development of certain rooms. In 1991 and 1992, Sonia Copeland Bloom gave gifts to equip a library IT room in memory of her husband, Harry Bloom, who passed away in 1981. Bloom was a Reader in the Department of Law, and a key thinker on the legal ramifications of digital technology and the developing World Wide Web. Although now an area of quiet study, the room remains commemorated in honour of Harry and his work.

SPECIAL COLLECTIONS

From its early days, the university library attracted many wonderful donations: all accessible today via the Special Collections reading room. By 1970, rare books and manuscripts were being given to the university for safe-keeping, future preservation and to allow wider access. The library received a collection of 18th-century books from a convent school in Hastings including a copy of Du Cange's Glossarium. A number of valuable texts were given from the estates of Major Teichmann Derville and Dr Gordon Ward, both local historians. Here we explore just a few of the distinctive collections housed in the university library and available for study by Kent students and researchers.

English Literature: The John Crow Collection

One of the earlier donations was John Crow's bequest of books and papers, amounting to around 12,000 unique items. John Crow was a Professor of English at the University of Pittsburgh, a lay theologian and a keen journalist, with a fondness for Elizabethan and Jacobean works of theatre. When he died in 1969, his collection was given to the University of Kent by Molly Mahood, a Professor in the English Department. It remains a popular resource for 17th-century sermons, Shakespeare plays and critiques, ballads, songs, proverbs and English language.

Politics: The Weatherill papers

Bruce Bernard Weatherill, known informally as Jack, was the Speaker of the House of Commons from 1983-1992 and famous for taking on the role against the wishes of the Prime Minister, Margaret Thatcher. He became a peer following his retirement. He lived for many years in Sevenoaks, Kent, and was involved in many community projects, including being vice-president of Kent Youth.[33] He received an honorary doctorate from the University of Kent in 1990.

The Weatherill Papers contain parliamentary and constituency papers from his political career, and also a fascinating collection of personal correspondence, family papers and an assortment of army manuals, guides and maps from Weatherill's period of service as a Captain in the 19th King George V's Own Lancers during the Second World War. After his death in 2007, further documents were deposited with the Templeman Library as part of his will.

Theatre: The Melville Collection

Brought together by Andrew Melville III and given to the university in the 1990s by his widow Joan Matheson, the Melville collection is a vast collection of theatre programmes, press cuttings, contracts, scripts, musical scores, photographs, advertisements and other documents relating to the once prolific theatrical family, the Melvilles. Headed by Andrew Melville III's grandfather George Melville, a Shakespearean actor, the family owned or leased over 25 theatres across Britain during the 18th and 19th centuries, and drew great acclaim for their pantomimes at the Lyceum Theatre in London. The 1,500-strong collection of documents was given to Kent due to the reputation of its Drama faculty, and the library's already enviable collection of theatre paraphernalia.

Local Figures: The Hewlett Johnson Papers

The Hewlett Johnson Papers are a collection of the sermon notes, photographs, correspondence, diaries, postcards and parish meeting minutes of Hewlett Johnson, the wartime Dean of Canterbury who held the post for over 30 years. The documents chart his experiences overseas in Russia, Spain and China, as well as his sympathy with communism, which led to his nickname, the 'Red Dean'. The collection also contains an autobiography detailing his meetings with historical figures such as Josef Stalin and Harry S. Truman. It was given to the University of Kent by members of his family.

Spiritualism: The Catherine Crowe Collection

The University of Kent received two legacy gifts of the novels and papers relating to the 19th-century writer on the supernatural, Catherine Crowe: one from Geoffrey Larkin, who was intending to write a biography of Crowe, and one from his researcher, Winifred Burgess. Crowe wrote *The Night Side of Nature, or, Ghosts and Ghost Seers*, a book that attempted to bridge the divide between scientific and fictional accounts of paranormal experience.

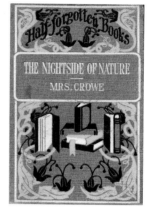

The collection contains articles about Crowe, Larkin's manuscript notes, scrapbooks of images relating to Crowe, and a number of correspondences from, to and about the writer. It also contains some of her most famous published works.

The Templeman library building opened in 1968. Today, it continues to grow and is currently undergoing a £12 million extension and a £10 million refurbishment. The early philanthropic gifts to the library, some of which are described above, are a key part of a history of philanthropy at Kent. In the next chapter, we look at how philanthropy is bound up with innovation and development, beginning with the university's two most novel archives – the British Cartoon Archive, and the brand new Stand-Up Comedy Archive.

Left The new Templeman library extension, opening 2015

5

INNOVATION
FORGING A PATHWAY FOR RESEARCH AND TEACHING

nnovation stands alongside excellence as a key feature of life at the University of Kent, and can be found not just in the academic disciplines, but also in daily practices across the campuses. This chapter details some of the ways that philanthropy has played a role in spurring innovation and progress across the campuses. It also looks at a few of the special relationships that make Kent distinctive.

ORIGINAL AND UNIQUE COLLECTIONS
THE BRITISH CARTOON ARCHIVE

An innovative addition to the University of Kent is the British Cartoon Archive, housed in the Templeman Library on the Canterbury campus. The Archive began in 1973, when the university established a Centre for the Study of Cartoons and Caricature – one of the first dedicated centres for the study of this genre in the United Kingdom. Dr Graham Thomas, a member of the politics department, had a longstanding interest in interwar polemical publications such as 'Penguin Specials'. Along with John Jensen, a political cartoon artist for the *Sunday Telegraph*, and Keith Mackenzie, Art Editor of Associated Newspapers, he established the first deposit of 20,000 original cartoons from the *Daily Mail* and the *Evening News*. The Nuffield Foundation provided £9,500 of funding for cataloguing later that year, which enabled staff in the newly-installed centre to begin the long process of archiving the items.

Above Cartoon by Richard Willson for *The Times*, 13 May 1987. British cartoon archive, 39784

Opposite page Rajvia Kaur's Elephant-Cow sculpture, winner of the Chancellor's Prize 2012

Many cartoonists donated their own unique works to the Centre, including Ernest Shepard and John 'Emmwood' Musgrave-Wood. The British Cartoon Association gave the works of Will Dyson from the *Daily Herald*. The Cartoon Editor of the *Daily Mirror*, Charles Roger, arranged for the work of more than a dozen artists to be acquired, including cartoon strips featuring the infamous 'Andy Capp'. Many original cartoons from the *Daily Express* were also given on loan from Beaverbrooks, including works by Sidney 'George' Strube, David Low, Michael Cummings and Victor 'Vicky' Weisz.[34]

From its conception, the Centre made it a policy not to purchase cartoons. Collections of original artwork are donated, or deposited on long-term loan with a proportion of the loan earmarked as an eventual donation. Some staff contributed gifts, such as a set of scarce 19th-century chromolithographs given by Professor Bryan Keith-Lucas in 1974. Research undertaken by staff at the Centre has attracted philanthropic grants from the Leverhulme Trust: a large grant in 1979 paid for two research fellows for three years, and another in 1982 paid for a study on the work of David Low. Another Leverhulme grant paid for research and a subsequent book about the 'Vicky' cartoons, culminating in an exhibition at the National Portrait Gallery in late 1987 to early 1988.

The Centre had many successful funding partnerships in the 40 years since it began, including with the Radcliffe Trust, the Pilgrim's Trust and the International Press Foundation. Support from the Maxwell Group for an exhibition and catalogue on 'De Gaulle through British Eyes' was unfortunately prematurely halted and never reinstated following Robert Maxwell's death in 1991.

Upon his death in 2005, the cartoonist Carl Giles bequeathed the entire collection of his work and papers to what was soon to become the British

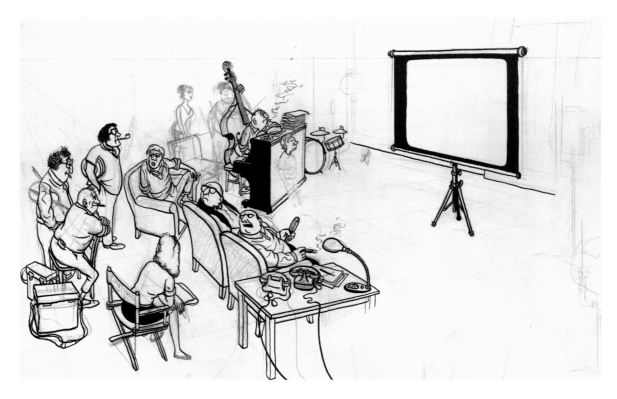

Cartoon Archive. His cartoon characters, including his 'Express Family', featured regularly in the *Daily Express* and the *Sunday Express* from 1943 to 1991. The archive now holds over 15,000 of Giles's cartoons and drawings, as well as 5,000 personal notes and letters.

The Centre became the British Cartoon Archive in 2007. Today, the collection comprises 140,000 pieces of original cartoon artwork, as well as 85,000 newspaper cuttings, and illustrated magazines, pamphlets and books. It collects up to 10 new cartoons every single day, which are deposited electronically by various newspapers as they are published.

The archive remains a unique and invaluable resource for the University of Kent, informing research not only on art, design and illustration styles, but also on political, social and economic British history. This material would have been inaccessible without the early philanthropic gifts to the archive, and the innovative spirit of the members of the Politics Department who helped develop it.

THE BRITISH STAND-UP COMEDY ARCHIVE

Established in 2013, the British Stand-Up Comedy Archive collects, preserves and celebrates material from those involved in this form of comedy. As part of the university's 50th Anniversary celebrations, the archive is being digitised in order to preserve the material in the long term as much of the collection is stored on obsolete analogue and digital audio-visual formats. Digitisation will also transform access to the collection for use in teaching and research, and for general enjoyment by as wide an audience as possible.

In 2013, the archive of Kent comedian Linda Smith (1958–2006) was deposited by her partner Warren Lakin. The gift included material from her childhood and university days, her early career as a stand-up comedian in the 1980s and 1990s, and her later career in radio and television. The archive contains notebooks, scripts, photographs, as well as audio-visual recordings of her contributions to the shows *Just a Minute*, *I'm Sorry I Haven't A Clue*, and *Have I Got News For You*.

Donations have also come from Tony Allen, a British Comedy Store regular and pioneering 'alternative' comic, who donated audio-visual recordings from his early career in the 1970s. Comedian and political activist Mark Thomas has donated props, audio-visual recordings, photographs, posters, press cuttings, and notes about his campaigns against the arms trade and multi-national corporations. Further offers of deposit have come from comedians Alexei Sayle, Jeremy Hardy, and Josie Long, as well as from others involved in the stand-up comedy scene, including comedy promoters and venues.

The British Stand-Up Comedy Archive supports University of Kent students studying for an MA in Stand-Up Comedy, and students opting for certain modules within the undergraduate degree in Drama and Theatre.

'The British Stand-Up Comedy Archive is unique in the world, and is as significant a venture as the university's establishment of the British Cartoon Archive forty years ago,' says Dr Nicholas Hiley, Head of Special Collections and Curator of the British Cartoon Archive. 'The British Cartoon Archive is the country's only other major archive of satirical humour, and, with stand-up comedy now the main form of political and social satire in Britain, the two archives will work together in collecting the records of satirical comment, and preserving them for current and future generations.'

> "
> We have an idea of what was going on in straight theatre hundreds or even thousands of years ago, because we can read the scripts of the plays that were performed. Stand-up comedy, on the other hand, always risks disappearing without trace.
>
> —Dr Oliver Double, Senior Lecturer and Head of Drama, University of Kent

© Steve Double

Left Mark Thomas and Linda Smith, 1989

This book is one of
the set of works by
T. S. Eliot
presented to Eliot College
by the directors of
Faber & Faber
in 1965, the year in which
the author died and the
College adopted his name.

Above First edition of
Selected Poems by
T. S. Eliot, donated by his
publisher, Faber & Faber

INNOVATIVE LECTURES

In October 1967 the poet W. H. Auden, a close contemporary of T. S. Eliot, gave the first Eliot lecture. The subject of the first lecture was martyrdom, and he discussed Eliot's work *Murder in the Cathedral*, a verse drama that portrays the assassination of Archbishop Thomas Becket in Canterbury Cathedral in 1170, which had been commissioned for the Canterbury Festival in 1935. Auden gave three lectures in total, which were funded by Faber & Faber, Eliot's publisher. Faber & Faber also funded some short courses on relevant themes, and published Auden's Eliot lectures in a book, *Secondary Worlds* (1968). The directors of Faber & Faber also donated several first editions of T. S. Eliot's poetry books to Eliot College, to commemorate his death in 1965.

Philanthropy also funded lectures on the subject of John Maynard Keynes, after whom the University of Kent's third college, built in 1968, was named. The seminars were the brainchild of Professor Robert Spence, the first Master of Keynes, who believed that Keynes ought to be commemorated in a similar way to Eliot by a series of lectures in his memory.[35] The Keynes Seminars were funded by Palgrave Macmillan, which also subsequently published them as books. They began with a lecture by Donald E. Moggridge in 1972 titled *Keynes: aspects of the man and his work*.

The Keynes Seminars continued until 1993, and many of Keynes's contemporaries attended over the years, including Roy Harrod, Richard Khan, Joan Robinson and Nicholas Kaldor.[36]

ESTABLISHING INNOVATIVE AREAS OF STUDY

In the early 1960s, the Nuffield Foundation made contact with each of the new universities to discuss how it might contribute towards any shortfalls the University Grants Committee could not cover. The Foundation suggested that, at Kent, it might be willing to fund a centre to study the history, philosophy and social relations of science. Professor Maurice Crosland was approached to lead as director of the interdisciplinary project, and in 1974, the Unit for the History, Philosophy and Social Relations of Science opened at Canterbury. Nuffield gave £95,000 to help toward salaries, books and the initial running costs for the Unit. In 1994, the Unit became the Centre for History of Cultural Studies of Science. It amalgamated with the Department of History, where research and teaching on the history of science, technology and medicine continues to this day.

> 'The need for a humanities-based, critical understanding of the nature of science, and its role in culture, is as strong as ever in the twenty-first century. In recent years it has become a research priority for funding bodies such as the Wellcome Trust. Thanks to the Nuffield Foundation's seed funding, Kent has led the way in this field ever since 1974, and is today an internationally recognised centre of scholarship in its current guise, the Centre for the History of the Sciences.'
> —Dr Charlotte Sleigh, Reader in the Department of History

The Pears family have donated a large amount of money to promote innovative research and teaching in the University of Kent's Centre for Philanthropy, which is part of the School of Social Policy, Sociology and Social

Research. Initially, they funded the costs of updating the much-acclaimed research report Why Rich People Give, by the Centre's Director Dr Beth Breeze and leading philanthropy author Theresa Lloyd. In 2014, the Pears Foundation also funded a three-year Pears Philanthropy Fellow post, to develop and teach the first MA in Philanthropic Studies to be available in the UK. This degree will be taught online using pioneering distance-learning methods targeted towards professionals working within the sector.

THE DURRELL INSTITUTE FOR CONSERVATION AND ECOLOGY (DICE)

Since it was founded in 1989, the Durrell Institute for Conservation and Ecology (DICE) has become the largest academic centre dedicated to conservation in the United Kingdom. This can be attributed in part to support from benefactors and foundations across the world, both for its research and for the development of teaching. DICE is based on the main Kent campus, and has strong ties to philanthropy at home and abroad, fostered by its agenda of campaigning for environmental awareness.

The Esmée Fairbairn Foundation has given over £100,000 to DICE. Other donors of note include Professor Ibnu Sutowo, Chair of the Wallacea Development Institute, who funded a chair in Biodiversity Management; and Dr Jonathan S. Swire, a doctor of molecular evolution who studied at Imperial College and has given over £100,000 to support staff and students at the Institute. Jonathan was continuing a family tradition of giving as his father, Sir John Swire, gave a generous donation to Kent in the 1990s to support overseas student scholarships.

DICE has its own charitable trust: the Durrell Trust for Conservation Biology. In addition, the Institute works in partnership with the International Union for Conservation of Nature, the Durrell Wildlife Conservation Trust, the United Nations Environment Programme's World Conservation Monitoring Centre, the Royal Botanical Gardens at Kew and the Powell-Cotton Museum in nearby Birchington.

Several Chairs relating to law and the environment have also been funded in the years since DICE opened its doors. Benefactors include the Kleinwort Charitable Trust (now CHK Charities), the trust of former banking house Kleinwort & Sons, which funded a chair in Environmental Law; and

> "
> The University of Kent has a warmer and more personal feel than bigger institutions. As a donor I feel appreciated for who I am as much as for what I give.
> —Robin Buxton

Left DICE staff

Cripps Harries Hall/SAUR UK, a law firm that funded a Chair in Wildlife Management Law. These initiatives were in partnership with Kent Law School.

Dr Robin Buxton, a former colleague of DICE's founder Dr Ian Swingland – who himself funds the Maurice Swingland prize for Masters students – has given over £200,000 via his own trust and the Patsy Wood Trust, a charitable organisation set up in honour of his sister. Dr Buxton's involvement with the university has grown since he first donated, and he is now involved in an advisory capacity as a DICE board member.

DICE is currently fundraising for 20 new scholarships to celebrate its 20th anniversary. The Institute also offers prestigious scholarships and prizes, including the Worcester Prize, set up by Sir Robert Worcester, the university's former Chancellor; and the Ellya Mustafa Award, which was created by DICE students and colleagues in memory of conservationist Ellya Mustafa, who died in 2011.

INNOVATION: A CHANCELLOR'S ROLE

One of the most important relationships for any university is with its Chancellor, the ceremonial figurehead who acts as the university's ambassador in the wider world. In 2007, the then Chancellor Sir Robert Worcester set up the Chancellor's Fund, emulating the generosity of the first Chancellor, Princess Marina, who gave £100,000 to the Foundation Fund. Sir Robert spent much of his early life in the United States, and strongly upheld the American view that fundraising is a central part of any university Chancellor's role. Sir Robert hopes that future Chancellors will continue to contribute toward the fund for years to come.

Below The Steinway grand piano in the Colyer-Fergusson Building's concert hall

PRINCESS MARINA, THE UNIVERSITY'S FIRST CHANCELLOR

Princess Marina was the wife of Prince George, the Duke of Kent, and aunt to the current Queen Elizabeth II. Born in Greece, her philanthropy was described as a consequence of her upbringing. Following the overthrow of the Greek Royal Family, she trained and worked diligently through the Second World War as a nurse.

Her Royal Highness Princess Marina, Her Majesty Queen Elizabeth II and the Queen Mother were, jointly, the largest independent donors to the first Foundation Fund at the University of Kent, giving £100,000 in total – equivalent to £1.3 million in 2015. Their names topped the First Benefactors List published in *The Times* in 1965.

Princess Marina agreed to take on the position of Chancellor in 1963 and undertook several visits to the early site prior to the university receiving its Charter. She was not formally installed in her role until 30 March 1966, when she, the then Lord Archbishop of Canterbury Dr Michael Ramsey, and John Haynes, the Secretary of the University Sponsors, received honorary doctorates and thus became the first official graduates of the University of Kent. Princess Marina served as Chancellor until her death in 1968.

Left Princess Marina at the graduation ceremony in 1968. The graduation thrones seen here, which have been used since the early days of the university, are also an example of philanthropy: they are a permanent loan from the Royal Commonwealth Society

At the time the Fund was established, Sir Robert said: 'I have set up a Chancellor's Fund, established to enable myself and my successors to put money wherever the Chancellors believe at the time it would be most useful.' The Fund was designed to support a range of university projects including music, academic scholarships and prizes. It was also used to purchase a Steinway grand piano for use in the Colyer-Fergusson Music Building.

INNOVATION: A BUSINESS ROLE

Partnerships with local and international businesses can incubate innovation, not least through the practice of industry placements. Over the past 50 years, Kent students have benefited from placements at BAE systems, Vodafone, Philips Research and Hewlett-Packard, among many other firms.

The School of Computing has a large undergraduate and taught MSc placement programme (120 students took a placement year in 2014/15), including an important relationship with Sun Microsystems, the computer company that invented Java, the programming language which runs on any computer. Students on a Sun placement scheme receive a full salary for a year and some work in the company's American offices. Sun Microsystems, and later Oracle, which acquired the company in 2010, have also donated computer hardware and supported the Computer Science department staff in the development of the Greenfoot and BlueJ open source software for teaching programming in schools and higher education.

This collaboration enabled many students to gain hands-on experience of using Java technology, thereby increasing their future employability. In 1998 the University of Kent became the first university in Europe to be recognised as an Authorised Academic Java™ Campus, reflecting the Computer Science department's first-rate reputation.

Kent's Computer Science department also has strong relationships with IBM and Microsoft. Research projects in the School have been supported through IBM Faculty Awards and a Microsoft Rotor grant. These awards have been mutually beneficial, to both the companies and academic researchers. For the companies, they have enabled their research staff to share new insights into the performance of modern programs; for the academics, the awards have provided resources that laid the foundations for successful applications to the UK Engineering and Physical Sciences Research Council for much larger projects.

The Science faculty has received support for innovative research and teaching since 1965, when Physics became the first discipline to have its own space on the brand-new Canterbury campus, in what is now the Marlowe building. Early gifts from companies such as Pfizer helped kick-start science research at Kent, and the relationship with industry has continued through many industry-funded innovations and scientific advancements.

In the 1990s, a partnership with Smiths Industries, a FTSE 100 technology company, supported the Pfizer contribution towards the Kent Institute of Medicine and Health Sciences. This research and development initiative involved medical professionals teaching practical and professional skills, alongside lecturing staff running more conventional academic courses. Smiths Industries also fund a number of studentships for the Institute.

Another partnership is provided by Santander Bank, which has a branch on campus. In 2012 Santander set up a scholarship fund to support students from Iberian and Latin American countries taking a Masters degree at the University of Kent. Santander has also helped with fundraising for the Law Campaign (see Chapter 6), participated in the Kent Business School Advisory Board, and funded the Santander Small to Medium Enterprise Internship Scheme with the aim of helping student employability. The bank funds the Staff and Student Mobility Awards, which allows recipients to immerse themselves in cultures overseas in order to enhance their educational and personal development.

A focus on innovation and potential has led Santander to join Kent Innovation and Enterprise in sponsoring the Big Ideas Competition. This offers budding student entrepreneurs support, advice, office space, the opportunity to compete in the Global Business Concept Challenge (an international competition held in Virginia, USA) and £1,000 towards a business start-up. The partnership with Santander brings many benefits to the university, not least in terms of access to global educational and organisational networks, especially in South American countries.

The development of lasting relationships with businesses has been a key part of the success of the University of Kent. Yet also crucial to this success has been engaging with the local community, not only through receiving funding or help from commerce, but also through offering support, volunteering, new opportunities and advice. The following chapter exemplifies some examples of engagement in Canterbury and beyond, and how the University of Kent has 'given back' to local people.

Below Santander fundraising for Kent Law Campaign

6

ENGAGEMENT
PHILANTHROPY ON AND OFF CAMPUS

As indicated in the earlier chapters, the University of Kent has been a grateful recipient of donations and help from the surrounding county. In return, the university has enriched the local area in many ways – not only with trade and employment (the university and its students contributed £0.6 billion to the South East region in 2009/10), but through shared creative endeavours, local activism, volunteer work, widening participation projects and access to legal advice.

Philanthropy is not a one-way system – it facilitates the bringing together of the university community and the city's residents. This chapter will demonstrate some of the ways this has happened, and the impact on both students and staff, and the local people.

> **" **
> There were things given in the early days, other than money, that I think were big contributions.
> —Robin Pitman, one of the first 500 students to study at Kent

CONNECTION 1: STUDENT JOURNALISM AND THE *KENT MESSENGER*

In 1965, the new University of Kent received a small donation of £100 from the *Kent Messenger,* a local newspaper. This donation, although low key and relatively small, marked the developing relationship between the newspaper and the university's students. The owner of the *Kent Messenger*, Mr Henry Roy Pratt Boorman, had sent a team led by his son Edwin to the university's campus with the aim of training-up the first intake of Kent student journalists. Over a weekend, Edwin Boorman and his team advised the new students on how to run a newspaper. As a result of this support, *inCant*, the first of Kent's student newspapers, was able to operate independently of university funding and of the newly-formed Kent Student Union.

Below Edwin Boorman (left) and H. R. Pratt Boorman of the *Kent Messenger*

Above *inCant* evolving over the years

inCant published a student perspective on various happenings on campus and beyond. The editorial team was led by founding students Robin Pitman and Richard Hoyle. Pitman remains grateful for the support provided by Mr Boorman and his newspaper:

> 'The inCants *are a clear indication of one of the major contributions that* Kent Messenger *and the Boorman family made to the university. Over that time,* inCant *was a really big thing in the university.* inCant *uniquely captured the zeitgeist of the new university.'*

inCant won several national awards, and ran for 20 years, with nearly 200 editions. It was the first foray into journalism for Gavin Esler, TV presenter and author, now the current Chancellor. BBC Radio presenter Mark Mardell also wrote for the paper during his years at the University of Kent.

H. R. Pratt Boorman's interest in student journalism at Kent was part of a wider vision. Five years before the university opened, Boorman had attended the International Weekly Newspaper Conference at Southern Illinois University in the United States. He was impressed with what he saw and wrote about his experience in the Newspaper Society monthly circular:

> 'In the United States, journalists' training is taken very seriously, they believe it is of tremendous value to their country and it is certainly raising the status and prestige of the weekly newspaper.
>
> 'Here in England we are shortly to found six new Universities... These six Universities are primarily for technical subjects but surely the Arts must not be overlooked, especially bearing in mind the growth of leisure of our people. The art of Journalism surely must not be overlooked.
>
> 'I think the weekly newspapers in England should consider very seriously whether some chair cannot be promoted in one of the new Universities in this country. Canterbury, where one of these six Universities is to be founded, is with London, Oxford and Cambridge, one of the oldest centres of printing in this country. The paper trade has already offered £100,000 to promote a Professor's Chair for papermaking technology.' —H. R. Pratt Boorman, Newspaper Society Monthly Circular, Sept/Oct 1960*

Boorman's granddaughter, Geraldine Allinson, the present chairman of the Kent Messenger (KM) Group, said of her grandfather, 'He was always very committed to his beliefs... It does not surprise me at all that he worked to try and find a way to fund a school for journalism in Canterbury.'

Boorman's vision of a School of Journalism at Kent was not realised until 2007. As the universities at Medway partnership was being formalised, Professor Tim Luckhurst, formerly of *The Scotsman* and the BBC, founded the Medway Centre for Journalism. Working in partnership with the *Kent Messenger*, the Centre secured an OFCOM Local Digital Terrestrial Programme Services licence to enable students to make local television in Kent. This will soon begin broadcasting to the Maidstone and Tonbridge area as *KMTV*, a local TV service with a proud 'county-centric' identity, from the University of Kent's Medway campus.

This venture joins the university's other local broadcaster, community radio station *CSRfm*. The station developed from *UKCRadio*, an AM station which was only available across the university's Canterbury campus, and is now a student-led community radio partnership between the University of Kent and nearby Canterbury Christ Church University. It is a far cry from the early days of student broadcasting when 'Audio Rutherford' and 'Audio Eliot' provided a rudimentary (and legal) campus radio broadcasting system that transmitted sound through amplifiers connected to the colleges' central heating systems.

> 'Much of the work KM Group does with the different communities and organisations in Kent is 'in kind' rather than through the simple provision of cash – the help given to the University of Kent when it started 50 years ago was no exception.
>
> 'I know that if my father and grandfather and their colleagues were here today they would be very proud to know that the Kent Messenger's *efforts to help the students at the University of Kent set up and run their own student newspaper are still remembered with such fondness. It is truly inspirational to me to see that their energy and drive 50 years ago made such an impact.'*—Geraldine Allinson, Chair of KM Group

This newspaper is printed by courtesy of Kent Messenger Ltd. Maidstone

Above Every edition of *inCant* paid homage to the *Kent Messenger* for the newspaper's assistance in printing, layouts and advice

CONNECTION 2: WOMEN'S STUDIES STUDENTS AND THE CANTERBURY WOMEN'S REFUGE

As the university approached its 10th birthday, the character of student activities changed. By the early 1970s, identity politics was looming large in the daily life of students and staff. Many women associated with the university attended 'consciousness-raising' discussions on the Canterbury campus, debating the problems created by a patriarchal society. This was feminism in its early form, as developed from the thinking around the first women's conference at Oxford University, and the first women's shelter, which opened in West London in 1971.

Below The Women's Centre on Stour Street, and some of the women and children housed there. *inCant*, April 27, 1976, p.4

In 1975, the student feminist group at the University of Kent announced that they were 'tired of talking', and determined to do something practical to help local women. They decided to set up a women's centre, and went about this by setting up a squat in a large building on Stour Street, near the social services building in Canterbury.

Jan Pahl, Emeritus Professor of Sociology who took part in the squat, describes what happened next:

> '*Almost immediately, women began to arrive. So these students, who thought they were going to set up a women's centre and offer pregnancy tests, support, and counselling on different things, and just a place for women to meet... they found there were all these abused women.*
>
> '*Then to their amazement, abused women came with children. I remember in the very early days a woman arrived barefoot in the middle of the night. She'd been beaten up by her husband and she'd walked from the village about six miles out, with her children.*'

Above The house on Stour Street today, which no longer houses the Women's Centre

Below Excerpt from the House Guidelines for the Women's Centre

As news about the Women's Centre spread, university staff and women from the local town turned up at the building to help the squat continue. One of those women was Sophie Scott, who had just moved to Canterbury in the spring of 1975. 'We got a letter through the door saying that some women had set up a Women's Centre and asking if we were interested in joining them,' she recalls. She was asked if she would help to 'hold the squat' by staying in the house for short periods of time to prevent repossession. 'What rapidly happened was, I would pick up my son from playgroup and we'd go straight back up the road to the Centre, and he'd play with the other children while I had a chat and helped out.'

THESE ARE NOT A SET OF RULES: THEY ARE GUIDELINES TO HELP MAKE THE RUNNING OF THE REFUGE EASIER FOR EVERYONE.

1. EACH WOMAN IS EXPECTED TO KEEP HER OWN ROOM/PART OF THE ROOM CLEAN AND TIDY AND TO JOIN IN WITH THE GENERAL WORK ROTA WHICH IS PINNED UP IN THE KITCHEN.

2. ALL WOMEN BUY AND COOK THEIR OWN FOOD AND FIND THEIR OWN STORAGE SPACE ? IF ANYTHING IS LEFT OUT ITS AT YOUR OWN RISK.

3. IF YOU GO OUT IN THE EVENING OR ANYOTHER TIME DURING THE DAY, MAKE SURE THAT YOU HAVE A BABYSITTER — THAT YOU ARE IN BY MIDNIGHT (WEEKDAYS) AND 1.00 (WEEKENDS) AND TO ENSURE THAT YOU TAKE SOME RESPONSIBILITY FOR YOU CHILDREN, THAT YOU ONLY GO OUT EVERY OTHER NIGHT, OTHER THAN WEEKENDS.

4. SO THAT WE CAN ALL GET SOME PEACE AND QUIET MAKE SURE THAT ALL CHILDREN ARE IN BED BY 7 IF THEY ARE UNDER 9 YEARS OLD AND 8 IF THEY ARE OVER 9 YEARS OF AGE.

Some students postponed their courses for a year and signed on the dole in order to keep the refuge going. As well as women's issues, members of the original group were concerned with squatters' rights, and addressing homelessness in the Canterbury area. An air of solidarity and a 'mutual relationship of support'[37] was fostered between the volunteers, the beneficiaries, and the community. Local people donated furniture, bedding, clothing, toys, even a Christmas tree and a turkey for Christmas dinner.[38] 'People gave all sorts of things,' said Sophie. 'They'd turn up with bundles of clothing, bundles of bedding, chairs, beds. One man handed us an envelope with £100 in notes in it. That paid for us to put a telephone in. We did have great resourcefulness, and a lot of help from all sorts of people.'

The distinction between those helping out at the refuge, and those being helped, was often blurred. One of the residents said at the time, 'They don't class you as a battered wife. They class you as a friend… [I]t's more like a home than being home.'[39] Sophie Scott agrees: 'You didn't make a distinction between "the people running the refuge" and "the victims". Everybody was just "a woman".'

By April 1976, 135 women and children had stayed at the refuge. The women were very active, running a local market stall to raise funds, and lobbying the local council and housing committee, often visiting Council members personally to persuade them to support the refuge. One woman set up an on-site shop of donated goods, where everything cost sixpence.

In November 1976, the Women's Centre was evicted from the building at Stour Street, and moved to a house offered by Canterbury City Housing Department in the village of Hersden outside Canterbury. The move was facilitated by *pro bono* legal advice offered by Professor Richard De Friend, Director of Kent Law School at that time, and Professor of Criminal Justice Steve Uglow, whose wife, Jenny Uglow, was actively involved in the Women's Centre. The Centre remained in Hersden until 1979, when it returned to the city, but this time to a legal site in Canterbury, where it remains.

The combined effort of activist students, staff and local women has provided services to women who are victims of abuse, and their families, for nearly 40 years in Canterbury. This story of philanthropy includes the philanthropic contribution of time, effort and goodwill made from people on campus to the local community, and would not be complete without paying homage to the passion and determination of these young students who were tired of simply 'talking' about women's rights.

Above Official opening of the new women's refuge in Canterbury in 1979

'The original philosophy of the students who set up our service continues in our organisation even to this day, 35 years later: we continue to provide services based on listening to the women and children who have survived domestic abuse. We always have, and still do ensure their needs are at the centre of all our decision-making.

'It is always essential that we do not forget the many areas of good practice and learning that have been developed over the years and we stand behind the desire to make a difference for the many victims and survivors of domestic abuse.' —Anne Lyttle, Director of Services at Rising Sun Domestic Violence & Abuse Service, which originated from the Canterbury Women's Refuge.

CONNECTION 3: KENT UNION AND LOCAL/ DISTANT COMMUNITIES

The University of Kent's student union ('Kent Union') is a major driver of the university's philanthropic efforts. Today, it is supported by over 2,700 volunteers,[40] employs over 600 paid staff, and is one of the UK's 500 largest registered charities. It enables the student community to 'give back' to the town of Canterbury and beyond.

Right Kent Union Awards 2014

© Kent Union

One of the main ways of giving back is through Kent RaG (Raise and Give), the main fundraising output of Kent Union, which raises money for a multitude of different causes on a local, national and international level. In 2013, RaG raised over £130,000 for charity.

Kent Union has a long track-record of charitable activity. One early project helped set up the Oaks Day Nursery on campus in 1969; this is now a charity administered under the Kent Union banner. Other projects include funding scholarships such as the South African Scholarship Fund, set up in the early 1980s to support black South Africans studying at the University of Kent, and hundreds of other volunteering ventures and Union-based charities.

Volunteering is one of Kent Union's biggest success stories. The Union offers students the opportunity to work towards the Kent Student Certificate for Volunteering (KSCV), for which students can log volunteer hours. 104,868 volunteer hours were logged in 2013/14, with over 38,000 of these being volunteer work in the local community. The number of student volunteer hours has seen a huge leap in the last five years:

	07–08	08–09	09–10	10–11	11–12	12–13	13–14
Student volunteer hours (per year)	30,930	28,843	36,791	46,146	82,000	103,964	104,868

'KSCV Platinum gave me the opportunity to understand how my volunteering had a positive impact on both the organisations I volunteered with as well as how I was developing from these experiences. The opportunity to learn more about the third sector and expand my knowledge on when and why people volunteer will allow me to have an advantage when I seek work in the third sector upon graduating.'
—Rory Murray: student volunteer

'Volunteering at the hospice since March 2013 has completely changed my outlook on life and I have discovered an overwhelming passion to study medicine. If I hadn't got involved in volunteering, my life may have still lacked direction and I certainly wouldn't be going off to study medicine in September. Volunteering in particular at the hospice has been amazing and I am so excited at the thought of one day being able to return to the place where my volunteering began, but as a doctor rather than a volunteer.'
—Alexandra Roy: student volunteer

Top Rory Murray
Bottom Alexandra Roy (right)

Union volunteers have worked with many locally-based charities, including the Kent-based homelessness charities Porchlight and Catching Lives, the Canterbury Foodbank, and Blythwood Care, as well as national and international organisations such as Children in Need, Age UK and Smile International. Students help in a wide variety of ways, from organising litter-picks to local gardening. On the University's Medway campus, Kent Union organises the Right to Read initiative, where volunteers go into a local primary school and read with the children, to improve their literacy and confidence.

Above Kent Union volunteers

In addition to local projects, Kent Union administers and helps several charities concerned with international issues:

- **A Village in Syria** is a student-led charity set up by politics students in 2013. Its aim is to improve the welfare and living conditions for displaced people in the Middle East: for example, by providing seeds to grow crops or wheat to make bread; diesel for tractors; money for water pumps, irrigation and polytunnels. The organisation is presently responding to the needs of people in conflict zones. It focuses on a particular village and IDP (Internationally Displaced Persons) camp in Syria: the normal population of around 500 people grew to 8,500 by July 2014, as vulnerable refugees fled civil unrest elsewhere.

  Whilst dealing with an ever-changing political situation in the Middle East, A Village in Syria has developed a sponsorship relationship with cosmetics company Lush; received *pro bono* legal advice from a lawyer (a Kent graduate himself); and has forged ties with a local artist who provided images from the village for an exhibition.

- **Seeds for Africa** is an independent charity, encouraging individuals and communities across Africa to be self-sufficient, by providing locally-sourced seeds, agriculture equipment, support and advice. It establishes orchards and vegetable gardens and works closely with primary schools to help them produce nutritious and reliable food. This year alone, it has provided training and advice for schools and households in Ghana, Sierre Leone, Uganda and Kenya.

Right Learning how to grow crops with Seeds for Africa

The University of Kent has built a partnership with the charity through its chairman Graham Holmes, who is also Director of Sport at Kent. The university provides office space and support services to the charity, and Kent Union volunteers help the campaigns.

- The university and Kent Union also support **Books To Africa**, a student-led group that raises funds and donations for the international organisation of the same name, which aims to distribute donated learning and teaching materials, funding and training to under-privileged schools and students in countries across Africa.
- **Kent Marrow** operates out of Kent Union, and raises funds and awareness on behalf of Anthony Nolan, the blood cancer charity. Set up by forensics student Katy Burnett, a former leukaemia sufferer, the charity works to recruit potential bone marrow and stem cell donors as well as fundraise for the cause.

CONNECTION 4: THE UNIVERSITY OF KENT AT MEDWAY, LOCAL HERITAGE AND WIDENING ACCESS

The University of Kent's £120 million Medway campus is part of the regeneration of Chatham Historic Dockyard. The siting of the new campus in this location was deliberately designed to make higher education more accessible to local communities, but it also contributes to local life through securing the future of historic sites and buildings. The Medway Partnership between the Universities of Greenwich, Kent and Canterbury Christ Church owes much to a philanthropic donation from the Rochester Bridge Trust, a charity that maintains the Rochester Bridge, promotes the bridge's heritage and makes grants to educational causes.

Above Students in the Pilkington Building, on the Medway campus

The University of Kent's Medway campus originated in a partnership with MidKent College, a further education college based in Chatham. In 1994, the college began offering courses that were accredited by the university, including a BSc in Social Science, Chemistry and Software Engineering, and an LLB in Law. Talks began between the two institutions and the Rochester Bridge Trust, and in December 1994 the Trust agreed to help the partnership between the university and college develop further by identifying 'a suitable building for lease or purchase'. Partnerships were also established with nearby Wye College and the Kent Institute of Art & Design, with the aim of forming a 'University for the Medway Valley'. All these institutions were offering vocational courses – finance, business, management, law and medicine – that complemented Kent's existing offer. These vocational disciplines were also attractive for their potential to unlock income from charity or industry sources.

The Rochester Bridge Trust offered one of its properties, the old Clock Tower building, to the university as a home for the Medway extension. Originally a naval storehouse built in 1723, this Grade II listed building was named the Bridge Warden's Study Centre, to mark the Trust's generosity in leasing the building rent-free.

In addition to waiving the rent, the Trust gave an initial grant of £350,000, to cover refurbishments, and later an additional £2,340,000 over seven years – substantially more than the £1,000,000 (£250,000 per year for four years)

THE ROCHESTER BRIDGE TRUST

The Rochester Bridge Trust was set up many centuries ago to maintain and repair an essential public amenity: similar trusts exist in many historic towns. In the case of Rochester, there are references to the bridge from as early as the 12th century. Rochester's bridge was destroyed and rebuilt many times over the centuries, all financed by the Trust's income from rents and charitable legacies. Today, two working bridges remain under the Trust's jurisdiction – a reconstructed Victorian bridge, completed in 1914; and a new bridge, built in 1970 for both road and rail traffic.

In the late 19th century, the Trust began to use its surplus funds to promote and support secondary education in the Medway area, with a particular focus on continuing girls' education. By the 20th century, it was also helping to develop higher education in the local area. In addition to its generous gift to the University of Kent in 1994, the Trust has supported various research projects, including the digitising of a project by the University of Kent's history department, looking at urban and agricultural rent from 1400–1914. It has also provided funding to other universities in Kent, with an aim of developing engineering research and knowledge.

The donation of the historically significant old clock tower building to the University of Kent made the Rochester Bridge Trust a member of the elite group of £1 million donors to the university.

Below The Bridge Warden's College (formerly the Bridge Warden's Study Centre and the Clock Tower building)

Above The Drill Hall Library

initially envisioned. The increase reflected the unforeseen costs of building alterations necessary to provide disabled access and new lecture theatre space. The Bridge Warden's College (as it was eventually renamed) opened in 1997. Later, it housed part of the university's Sociology, Social Policy and Social Science Research department. In 2015, the building remains in use as part of the School of Arts.

By 2005, the University of Kent was continuing to grow, and expanded to a site at Chatham Maritime, the historic dockyard at the mouth of the River Medway. The location had a rich history, as illustrious as that of the University of Kent's original site at Canterbury; but more importantly, it had rich potential for the future. It was perfectly placed to provide higher education to the Medway region, traditionally a low-intake area for universities.

The new campus injected new life into the old naval site. New buildings were erected and the historic buildings were renovated to make them fit for their new purpose.

One historic building is now the Drill Hall Library. The original Drill Hall at the Royal Navy Barracks at Chatham was decommissioned in 1984. Built in 1902, the complex was the base for HMS Pembroke, for many years. Following its closure, the Grade II listed buildings were refurbished for use by the three Medway Partnership universities. The £3.3 million refurbishment was not funded by philanthropy, but by the South East England Development Agency (SEEDA); yet the Drill Hall Library contains many donated objects relating to its naval history.

Below 'Dead Man's Penny'

The widow of Arthur Voice, a serviceman who was killed in 1917 during an air raid on the barracks, gave the library his Bible and his 'Dead Man's Penny', a medal sent to relatives of those who died during the First World War. Other donations include: a collection of photos and a Newfoundland flag, given by a relative of Thomas Ginn, another air raid victim; and photographs of Archibald Hay, the youngest man to die in the air raid on the Drill Hall by German Gotha bombers in 1917. Here, philanthropy helps the compelling history of this building be remembered.

CONNECTION 5: THE KENT LAW CAMPAIGN, THE LEGAL PROFESSION, AND SERVING THE COMMUNITY

In 2009/2010 the University of Kent set itself an ambitious £5 million fundraising target to build a bigger home for the Kent Law Clinic and a new Moot Court, part of the Kent Law School.

Professor Joanne Conaghan, head of Kent Law School at the time, set the ball rolling for the Law Campaign by identifying a number of people who might be willing to contribute to a new Law building, including people who had already invested in the School of Law and were excited for its future prospects. Many went on to become donors, and eventually Board members. A group of Patrons were recruited – well-connected ambassadors, mostly from the legal profession; as well as a student group and a Young Alumni group. All were committed to raising support and money. Professor Richard De Friend, a Kent Law alumnus who enjoyed strong relations within the professional law community, was appointed Chair of the Campaign.

By 2011, the Law Campaign had moved into its 'Quiet Phase', the period prior to the campaign kick-off, building foundations through starting conversations with donors, drumming up alumni support and involving students. In 2012, Hilary Edridge, Head of Campaigns and Anna Pollard, Campaigns Manager in the Development Department at the University of Kent, rolled out their programme of alumni events: lectures in both London and Canterbury, informal pub nights, formal networking receptions and sponsored events. The London lectures were delivered by high-profile legal luminaries, including The Rt Hon Lord Justice Goldring and The Rt Hon Sir James Munby.

The Law Campaign received some very generous gifts as a result of these efforts. Dr Kennedy Wong, an alumnus from Hong Kong, gave £500,000 to the campaign, and will have a mooting chamber named in his honour. He has also supported the university's Hong Kong Alumni Scholarship Fund.

In the summer of 2013 The Hon Charles Wigoder, a Kent alumnus, entrepreneur and philanthropist made a gift of £1 million towards the Campaign, which was one of the largest single donations from an individual ever received by the university. His decision to give over £1 million towards the Law Building catapulted the Law Campaign into the 'public' phase, which was launched at a glittering event in London, held at the top of 30 St Mary Axe – the building known as the 'Gherkin' – on 6 November 2013.

WHAT THE LAW CLINIC DOES

The Kent Law School houses the Law Clinic, which was first launched in 1972; the first of its kind in the country. The Clinic allows students to work alongside qualified barristers and solicitors to provide *pro bono* legal services to local communities in Kent. Due to Canterbury's proximity to Dover, there is also a pressing need for legal support for those seeking asylum: several charities operate in the county to assist refugees, whether entering the UK or facing deportation.

In early 2014, the Law Clinic won a landmark human rights case for an Afghan man who was due to be deported. As an atheist, he was sure that if he returned to his home country he would be persecuted for renouncing his

Below Dr Kennedy Wong

THE HONORABLE CHARLES WIGODER

Charles Wigoder graduated from the University of Kent in 1978, having studied Law and Accountancy. He subsequently qualified as a chartered accountant with KPMG in 1984 and worked as an investment analyst with Kleinwort Securities. He went on to become a successful entrepreneur in the telecoms and energy markets, initially with Peoples Phone and most recently with Telecom Plus (trading as the Utility Warehouse Discount Club). In 2009, he was given an honorary doctorate by the then Chancellor of the university, Sir Robert Worcester.

At the public launch of the Law Campaign, Charles gave a moving speech about his decision to support the campaign with a £1 million donation. His father had been an eminent lawyer and political activist, and was involved in a number of major civil rights cases during the 1960s and 70s. While not a lawyer himself, Charles is a committed philanthropist who runs his own eponymous charitable foundation, supporting a wide range of causes with a focus on improving educational access, facilities and standards. His gift to the Law Campaign was not only to give something back to his alma mater, but to honour the inspirational and dedicated work of his late father.

Above Law students competing in the final of the Crown Prosecution Service Moot 2012

religion and sentenced to death under Sharia Law. This is believed to be the first time that the United Kingdom has granted asylum to an applicant who as an atheist feared persecution 'for reasons of religion' within the meaning of the 1951 UN Refugee Convention.

Recent cuts to legal aid in Britain have meant an increase in demand for the Law Clinic's services. Already the Clinic has to turn people away, says Anna Pollard, Law Campaign manager. But with the new building, many more students can work on cases at any one time, and in that way help many more people.

Despite being unlikely to benefit personally from the new building which will be complete in 2016 after many of the student group have graduated, they have worked tirelessly in raising money for the campaign and have contributed an immense effort. The Law Campaign Student Group began in 2011–2012, and was formalised in 2012–2013 as a Kent Union 'volunteering society'. The group has won numerous fundraiser awards, and raised £17,000 last year through sponsored runs, swims, marathons, skydives, abseils and bungee-jumps.

Law is a competitive discipline, making volunteering attractive as a means to gaining additional skills and experience. 'We have to make sure that our students have got something that sets them apart,' says Anna Pollard. 'You can only learn so much from a textbook, so to take on real-life cases is really important.' As part of their courses, students have the opportunity to work at the Law Clinic, which gives them a practical understanding of the process of law. The experience offers students other benefits too including, employability skills, access to professional networks and personal development. Students undertake a range of tasks including staffing the reception and answering the phones, interviewing clients, drafting legal documents, corresponding, and undertaking legal research into case and statute law relevant to the case. Some get the opportunity to negotiate or advocate (under supervision) on behalf of clients, giving them valuable experience whilst enabling them to give something back.

Right Law Campaign Student Group 5km Fun Run in 2013

'In Hong Kong we don't have these kinds of opportunities. That's the reason why I joined the Law Campaign, and why I did other volunteering as well: to make my Uni experience more fun and more colourful, and to do something to help.' —Billy Ng, Vice-President of Kent Law Campaign Student Group

The students and the Young Alumni group, made up of recent law graduates, have raised over £50,000 for the new Law building. Since hitting this target, they have set themselves a new fundraising target of £75,000.

The new Wigoder Law Building is due to be completed in 2016. Located next to Eliot College, it will enjoy a beautiful view out to Canterbury and the Cathedral.

The Kent Law Campaign has been shortlisted for the 'Outstanding Development/Alumni Relations Team' Prize in *The Times* Higher Education Leadership and Management Awards, 2015, in recognition of its strong engagement capacity and its ability to galvanise support from many different groups.

The campaign has engaged law alumni, current students and friends of the university in a range of fundraising initiatives, and also drawing in many individuals and organisations in the local community behind the university and the Law Clinic. It demonstrates the importance of engagement beyond the university campus, and how reciprocal relationships have helped the university, not only in terms of income, but also to embed it within the wider community in which it resides.

The Law Campaign, along with the other examples shown here, emphasises how communication, cooperation and reciprocation have helped to develop the university. The final chapter will show how this form of engagement is one of three main strategies for future philanthropy at the University of Kent.

Above Billy Ng skydiving to raise money for the Law Campaign

Below Artist's impression of the Wigoder Law Building, designed by architects Hawkins\Brown

7 ENDOWMENT

LOOKING TO THE FUTURE

The history of philanthropy at the University of Kent may be hidden, but it has left an enduring legacy. Donations from friends and associates, former students and staff, local residents and eminent Kent people have underpinned the university's values, helped students who might not otherwise have completed their studies and accumulated valuable collections that enhance Kent's unique identity. Philanthropy has helped mark Kent's character as an institution with strong connections, memories and resources.

In 2013, the *Coutts Million Pound Donor Report*, researched and written by staff in the Centre for Philanthropy at Kent, reported that for the first time in the United Kingdom, universities received more large gifts than any other charitable cause.[41] In recent years, UK universities have tended towards scaling-up their philanthropic efforts, taking alumni relations and donor development more seriously. Spurred by the introduction of HEFCE's match funding scheme in 2008, which aimed to boost fundraising in institutions by matching donations pound for pound, philanthropic gifts to higher education reached an all-time high of £657 million in 2014–15.[42] It has been estimated that, by 2022, philanthropic income to higher education institutions could rise to as much as £2 billion a year from over 640,000 different donors.[43]

However, most of the largest philanthropic gifts are given to Oxford and Cambridge – these two ancient universities accounted for over half of the total philanthropic higher education income in 2012/13, leaving all the other universities including Kent to share the other half. A future vision for philanthropy at the university, drawing upon the 'hidden history' that has been laid out in this book, is suggested here. It boils down to three simple goals: more philanthropy; more engaged philanthropy, and more international philanthropy.

MORE PHILANTHROPY

Since 2010, the University of Kent has generated over £9 million in philanthropic income.[44] The university has learnt from and built on its past experiences since the first fundraising appeal; enabling the building of prestigious sports facilities, a unique music building, a popular community theatre, and numerous departmental buildings, all supported by philanthropic donations.

Below Deputy Vice-Chancellor Professor Keith Mander

One of the key objectives for the future at Kent is to drive and sustain institutional advancement. In order to do this, investment in fundraising capacity is essential: fundraising must become a core part of the university's mission.

> '*I believe there is particular pleasure to be had from making a philanthropic contribution to, for example, enable an individual to do something that they could not afford on their own, and for multiple donors to contribute to something that none of them could afford to fund individually.*' —Professor Keith Mander, Deputy Vice-Chancellor and Chair of Fundraising Co-ordination Committee

In the next 10 years, the University of Kent is hoping to launch a new major campaign to raise funds for capital projects – including new buildings, garden spaces and squares – and for research and student support. The hope is that the campaign will be supported by an increase in alumni-giving, a

diversification of income streams, the enhancing of local relationships with industry and the community, and a move toward the established American-style model of higher education funding. All this is a positive response to the 'era of uncertainty' in the 1970s and 1980s, which saw an abrupt and severe curtailment of government funding for higher education.[45] The new vision will require a scaling-up of resourcing for fundraising and alumni relations, as this results in demonstrable growth in philanthropic income.[46]

'We have a vision for the future of the university that incorporates philanthropy at its very core, rather than as a nice addition to government funding. This will involve a drive to raise more funds across the board – not only for large capital projects, like we have had in the recent past, but also for unrestricted funds that can be then allocated to the area of most need' —Alison Coles, Director of Development at the University of Kent

The university's role in its local community and the rest of Kent cannot be underestimated. As with any other major organisation, it provides employment and generates income and wider benefits for the local area. In 2012/2013, the university generated £0.7 billion for the regional economy, with the students alone contributing £249 million by relying on local goods and services such as accommodation and retail. It supplies nearly 6,000 jobs in the regional community.[47]

The University of Kent remains one of the largest employers in the county, and as has been shown, works closely with local businesses and charitable organisations. The role these relationships play in town-and-gown cooperation is important for future potential fundraising.

Above Alison Coles

MORE ENGAGED PHILANTHROPY

Sometimes described as 'strategic' or 'venture' philanthropy, in the context of the University of Kent, 'engaged philanthropy' refers to:

- High levels of engagement between the donor and the recipient institution. Rather than being simply a source of finance, the benefactor remains involved in the project they help fund, adding the benefit of their skills, knowledge and intellectual vigour.
- Strategic and targeted use of money, a process that adopts some of the characteristics of a business model to measure and predict outcomes, in order to ensure that funds are focused in ways that are most useful.
- Strengthening local and international networks, including industry and personal connections.

The practice already exists at Kent, particularly where donors have been successful in business. These donors are interested in active participation at an advisory level with the university. Paul Dyer, the alumnus who founded the Towergate Partnership insurance company, has not only given gifts of money to the university. He also offers students the opportunity to take part in his leadership enhancement programme with Kent Business School, has served on the *ad hoc* committee for the extension of the Templeman Library, and also set up an Advancement Committee for Kent Business School, concerned with raising money to help the school to prosper. He says of engaged philanthropy, 'Individuals who give want to see a specific output. I know exactly where my money is going; I know the students I sponsor in Archaeology and in History. I get much more fun and personal benefit from being hands-on.'

Other examples of donors directly involved with projects include Dr Robin Buxton, who is on the Advisory Board for the Durrell Institute of Conversation and Ecology, where he employs his expertise as a Chartered Environmentalist, and his experience with numerous conservation organisations around Oxfordshire. Dr Garry Rogerson is a Biochemistry alumnus who has contributed significantly to the Stacey Fund, which helps students from low-income families by providing opportunities for practical work experience in laboratories. Coming from a management background, Dr Rogerson's gift was set up to be a 'challenge gift', encouraging other Stacey Fund donors to contribute.

Above Paul Dyer

HOW DO WE ACHIEVE MORE ENGAGED PHILANTHROPY?

....

'Firstly, we need specific propositions that people feel compelled to support. These propositions might centre on providing beneficial support for individual students, or replicating a positive experience that the donor themselves had. On a larger scale, a proposal might perpetuate a name for posterity, or provide the capital for new academic endeavour.

'Secondly, good propositions need to be located within the university's wider mission. A donor may willingly support a small initiative in a small way, but for a larger donation, the donor needs to be confident that the university is, and will remain, committed to the proposition, at least for enough time to allow the benefits of the proposition to be felt. Many levels of support and reassurance may be needed, perhaps by many different people, perhaps over a long period.

'Thirdly, we need to communicate passionately the value of the proposition, and the difference that philanthropic support will make. "People give to people" not only means that people will give to help people; it also means that people will give if the right person asks them. It is about more than a bald recitation of facts, but about articulating a motivational narrative that leads to action – in particular, the action of making a philanthropic donation.

'Finally, we need to invest in stewardship as well as solicitation. Donors can themselves be powerful advocates for other donors, so involving donors in seeing the direct impact of their donations, through invitations to events, or involving them in advisory boards, encourages them to be independent advocates for the cause that they have supported.'
—Professor Keith Mander

“
The university represents a blank sheet of paper with colossal potential. It is a staggering resource. What's key is harnessing the intellectual talent we have inside the University of Kent.
—Paul Dyer, donor

Partnerships with these individuals are crucial, but they are not the only option for effective philanthropy. In 2013/14, gifts from organisations accounted for 56% of all gifts to UK higher education institutions.[48] The university is working more closely with charitable foundations and corporate donors. While one-off gifts from foundations are more usual – for example, the Shumei Foundation in the 1990s donated £120,000 to fund a Chair in International Relations of East Asia – there are many examples of longer-term funding. One is the Pears Foundation's connection to the university's Centre for Philanthropy, which has been sustained over several years because of the Foundation's active interest in understanding and encouraging charitable giving. Funding from large charitable trusts like the Leverhulme Trust and the Wellcome Trust are also, of course, examples of effective philanthropy where the donor takes a keen interest in outcomes.

MORE INTERNATIONAL PHILANTHROPY

Higher education has become increasingly globalised, and universities are no longer solely operating in a local or national market.

The University of Kent has been at the forefront of a sector-wide move towards building connections overseas. Forty per cent of Kent's staff come from outside the UK; 4,530 students from 140 countries are currently studying here. Alumni in 200 countries across the globe are still in touch with the university.[49] For the 50th anniversary, alumni celebrations are taking place all over the globe, from Kuala Lumpur to India, Nigeria to Italy.

Above Hong Kong alumni

As the original university at Canterbury has extended internationally, so too have its activities around philanthropy. As discussed in Chapter 4, numerous scholarships and research are funded by alumni groups and individuals across the globe. A recent £500,000 pledge from a donor in the Middle East has just been received to support a new building for Kent Business School. As a result, new fundraising networks are opening up for the university in the Middle East, supplementing the already strong links with East Asia, through the Hong Kong China Portal. The University of Kent has alumni groups in America, and partnerships with charities and companies in Europe.

'Many of our US-based alumni make two observations about studying at Kent. First, that coming to Kent gave them (or reinforced in them) a "world view" that broadened their horizons physically and emotionally. Second, that coming to Kent was a life-defining experience, opening up to them new possibilities and new ideas that subsequently defined highly successful careers.

'These alumni need no persuading that Higher Education is A Good Thing, because they recognise it on a daily basis. Despite having an excellent Higher Educational system in their own country, they took a brave step to sample a new country and a new culture, and were consciously enriched by the experience.' —Professor Keith Mander

The University of Kent's Mission Statement up to 2015 incorporates a strong drive towards internationalisation. Alongside the importance of 'innovative and world-leading research', the Mission Statement emphasises the need to have a 'positive impact regionally, nationally and especially internationally'. These impacts are growing not only through the work of the university, but also through its strong alumni connections, particularly in America and South East Asia.

The future plan is for the university to develop these and continue to recruit more alumni overseas. This will open up opportunities not only for income, but also to secure more student placements offered by international alumni and partnership organisations and, by using crowdfunding, combine the power of the Internet and broad international networks to allow engagement with donors all around the world.

PHILANTHROPY: A NEVER-ENDING HISTORY
This book has discussed 50 years of the 'hidden history' of philanthropy at the University of Kent. As that history develops, we can hope that it will become less hidden. The changing landscape of higher education funding requires philanthropy to become ever more prominent within the university's operations. Every day, regular gifts are received, new partnerships are formed, new donations are given, and so the story continues. This book pays tribute to the many people and organisations that have contributed to the University of Kent, from the first promise of land for the site back in 1960 up to the present day, gifts that commemorate 50 glorious years.

"
I do it...
because I love
the university.
—James Bird, donor,
on why he gives.

Below University
of Kent graduates

ENDNOTES

1. Squire, W. (2014) *University Fundraising in Britain: A Transatlantic Partnership.* London: Matador, p3.
2. Robbins, L. C. (1963) *Higher Education: Report of the Committee appointed by the Prime Minister under the Chairmanship of Lord Robbins, 1961–63.* London: HMSO, p15.
3. *Ibid.*, p260.
4. Kent Further Education Sub Committee (1960) *Meeting notes.* T60/10, Canterbury: University of Kent Library Archives, p5.
5. Barnes, L. (2011) 'Education and Training.' in *Social Trends 41.* London: Office for National Statistics, p17.
6. Carpentier, V. (2004), Historical Statistics on the Funding and Development of the UK University System 1920–2002, Colchester, Essex: UK Data Archive, [online] Available at: http://discover.ukdataservice.ac.uk/catalogue/?sn=4971&type=Data%20catalogue [Accessed 12/11/2014]
7. More Partnership (2012) 'Review of Philanthropy in UK Higher Education.' *Higher Education Funding Council for England (HEFCE). September 2012*, p5.
8. Squire, W. (2014) *University Fundraising in Britain: A Transatlantic Partnership.* London: Matador, p4.
9. Browne, J. (2005) 'Presidential address commemorating Darwin.' *The British Journal for the History of Science, 38 (3), 251–274,* p262.
10. Martin, G. (1990) *From Vision to Reality.* Canterbury: University of Kent at Canterbury, p103.
11. Calouste Gulbenkian Foundation (2010) *Calouste Sarkis Gulbenkian – the man and his work.* Lisbon: Armenian Communities Department, p36.
12. Bann, S. *et al.* (1992) *Sculpture on the Campus.* Canterbury: University of Kent at Canterbury, pp3–4.
13. Martin, G. (1990) *From Vision to Reality.* Canterbury: University of Kent at Canterbury, p228.
14. Green, C. (1995) 'Heroes: Peter Stone.' *Kent Magazine.* Canterbury: University of Kent at Canterbury, p9.
15. Martin, G. (1990) *From Vision to Reality.* Canterbury: University of Kent at Canterbury, p192.
16. Templeman, G. (1971) *Sixth Report of the Vice-Chancellor.* Canterbury: University of Kent at Canterbury, p24.
17. Cork, R. (2003) *Breaking Down the Barriers: Art in the 1990s.* New Haven: Yale University Press, p545.
18. Martin, G. (1990) *From Vision to Reality.* Canterbury: University of Kent at Canterbury, p106.
19. *Ibid.*, p193.
20. Beloff, M. (1968) *The Plate Glass Universities.* London: Secker & Warburg, p140.
21. Templeman, G. (1962) Notes, 22nd September 1962. Kent Foundation Appeal. Canterbury: University of Kent Library Archives.
22. Syers, C. (1964) *Letter to Appeal Committee, 5th October 1964.* Appeal Current. Canterbury: University of Kent Library Archives.
23. The Working Committee of the Appeal Committee (1964) *Notes from the First Meeting, 29 December 1964*, Main Appeal 1st File. Canterbury: University of Kent Library Archives, p3.
24. Syers, C. (1965) *Meeting notes from press visit, 24th May 1965,* 2 June 1965. Appeal Current. Canterbury: University of Kent Library Archives.
25. The Working Committee of the Appeal Committee (1965) 'Broadcasting the Appeal through Kent', *Paper #4,* 19 February 1965. Main Appeal 1st File. Canterbury: University of Kent Library Archives.
26. Templeman, G. (1966) *First Report of the Vice Chancellor June 1966.* Canterbury: University of Kent at Canterbury.
27. The documents in the University of Kent Library Archives do not state an official final figure nor end date for the University

Foundation Fund Appeal – the final mention of it is in August 1966, when a third subscription list was published in *The Times* (12 August 1966, p7). The appeal total has been described by Graham Martin in *From Vision to Reality* (1990, Canterbury: University of Kent at Canterbury, p217) as "rather less than £750,000", while Michael Shattock (in *Making a University: a Celebration of Warwick's First Twenty-Five Years,* [1991] Coventry: University of Warwick) gives the final appeal total for Kent as £600,000.

28.   Beloff, M. (1968) *The Plate Glass Universities.* London: Secker & Warburg, p.53.

29.   King, P.G. (1970) 'Progress and Developments in the Library of the University of Kent at Canterbury'. *Masters in Arts thesis.* University of Loughborough, p11–13.

30.   *Ibid.,* p44.

31.   Templeman, G. (1967) *Second Report of the Vice Chancellor, June 1967.* Canterbury: University of Kent at Canterbury, p18.

32.   King, P.G. (1970) 'Progress and Developments in the Library of the University of Kent at Canterbury'. *Masters in Arts thesis.* University of Loughborough, p43.

33.   Kent Online (2007) 'Ex-speaker had many Kent Connections' [Online] Available at: www.kentonline.co.uk/kent/ news/ex-speaker-had-many-kent-connect- a29629/ [Accessed 29/01/15]

34.   Seymour-Ure, C. (1997) *A Sense of Permanence: Essays on the Art of the Cartoon.* Canterbury: Centre for the Study of Cartoons and Caricature, p9.

35.   Crabtree, D. and Thirlwall, A. P. (eds.) (1993). *Keynes and the Role of the State: The Tenth Keynes Seminar Held at the University of Kent at Canterbury, 1991.* London: Palgrave Macmillan, pxii.

36.   Arestis, P. and McCombie, J. (2006). 'Introduction.' In Arestis, P. & McCombie, J. and Vickerman R. (eds.) *Growth and Economic Development: Essays in Honour of AP Thirlwall.* Cheltenham: Edward Elgar Publishing, p2.

37.   Pahl, J. (1978) *A Refuge for Battered Women. Department of Health and Social Security.* London: HMSO, p4.

38.   *Ibid.,* p6.

39.   *Ibid.,* pp50–1.

40.   University of Kent (2014) *Financial Statements 2014,* Canterbury: University of Kent, p9.

41.   Breeze, B. (2013) *The Coutts Million Pound Donors Report.* London: Coutts.

42.   NatCen / Council for Advancement and Support of Education (2015) 'Giving to Excellence: Generating Philanthropic Support for UK Higher Education.' *Ross-CASE Report 2013-14.* London: NatCen, p2.

43.   More Partnership (2012) 'Review of Philanthropy in UK Higher Education' *Higher Education Funding Council for England (HEFCE). September 2012,* p3.

44.   University of Kent Development Office (2015) *Catalysing Change: 2015/16 Annual Plan & 10 Year Income Growth Plan.* Canterbury: University of Kent.

45.   Cook, W. B. (2008) 'Fundraising and the College Presidency in an Era of Uncertainty: From 1975 to the present' in Walton, A. & Gasman, M. (eds.) *Philanthropy, Volunteerism and Fundraising in Higher Education.* Boston, MA: Pearson, p626.

46.   NatCen / Council for Advancement and Support of Education (2015) 'Giving to Excellence: Generating Philanthropic Support for UK Higher Education', *Ross-CASE Report 2013-14.* London: NatCen.

47.   University of Kent (2015) *Regional Impact: Making a Difference.* Canterbury: University of Kent Corporate Communications, p4.

48.   NatCen / Council for Advancement and Support of Education (2015) 'Giving to Excellence: Generating Philanthropic Support for UK Higher Education', *Ross-CASE Report 2013-14.* London: NatCen, p22.

49.   University of Kent (2015) *Regional Impact: Making a Difference.* Canterbury: University of Kent Corporate Communications, p4.

FURTHER READING

This book owes a great deal to the documents in the University of Kent Library Archives, particularly those relating to the foundation of the university. The author also recommends the following titles on philanthropy and higher education:

- James Andreoni (2006). 'Philanthropy'. In Kolm *et al.* (eds.) *Handbook of the economics of giving, altruism and reciprocity*, *2*, 1201-1269
- Michael Beloff (1968) *The Plate Glass Universities*. London: Secker & Warburg
- Mathew Bishop & Michael Green (2008) *Philanthrocapitalism: How giving can save the world*. New York: Bloomsburg Press
- Beth Breeze & Theresa Lloyd (2013) *Richer Lives: Why Rich People Give*. London: Directory of Social Change
- Peter Frumkin (2006) *Strategic Giving: the art and science of philanthropy* Chicago: Chicago University Press
- Amy Kass (ed.) (2007) *Giving well and doing good*. Bloomington, IN: Indiana University Press
- Graham Martin (1990) *From Vision to Reality*. Canterbury: University of Kent at Canterbury
- David Owen (1965) *English Philanthropy 1660–1960*. Oxford: Oxford University Press
- Robert Payton & Michael Moody (2008). *Understanding philanthropy: Its meaning and mission*. Bloomington, IN: Indiana University Press
- William Squire (2014) *University Fundraising in Britain: A Transatlantic Partnership*. London: Matador
- Andrea Walton & Marybeth Gasman (eds.) (2008). *Philanthropy, Fundraising, and Volunteerism in Higher Education*. Boston: Pearson

CENTRE FOR PHILANTHROPY, UNIVERSITY OF KENT
A leading centre of philanthropy research, teaching and public engagement
www.kent.ac.uk/sspssr/philanthropy

ALLIANCE
The leading magazine for philanthropy and social investment worldwide
www.alliancemagazine.org

COUNCIL FOR ADVANCEMENT AND SUPPORT OF EDUCATION (CASE)
Support for advancement professionals in educational institutions
www.case.org

PHILANTHROPY IMPACT
Inspiring philanthropy and social investment across borders, sectors and causes
www.philanthropy-impact.org